W9-BMJ-663

Polished Spiral Karin Kuhlmann

"Although the creation of fractals is bounded to strict mathematical rules, the results are always very inspiring."– **Karin Kuhlmann**

Student Math Handbook

Investigations

IN NUMBER, DATA, AND SPACE®

Editorial offices: Glenview, Illinois • Parsippany, New Jersey • New York, New York
Sales offices: Boston, Massachusetts • Duluth, Georgia
Glenview, Illinois • Coppell, Texas • Sacramento, California • Mesa, Arizona

The Investigations curriculum was developed by TERC, Cambridge, MA.

This material is based on work supported by the National Science Foundation ("NSF") under Grant No.ESI-0095450. Any opinions, findings, and conclusions or recommendations expressed in this material are those of the author(s) and do not necessarily reflect the views of the National Science Foundation.

ISBN: 0-328-24091-5

ISBN: 978-0-328-24091-3

9 10-V082-15 14 13 12 11 10 09

CC:N2

Math Words and Ideas

Number and Operations

Patterns, Functions, and Change

Data and Probability

Geometry and Measurement

Games

The ***Student Math Handbook*** is a reference book. It has two sections.

Math Words and Ideas

These pages illustrate important math words and ideas that you have been learning about in math class. You can use these pages to think about or review a math topic. Important terms are identified and related problems are provided.

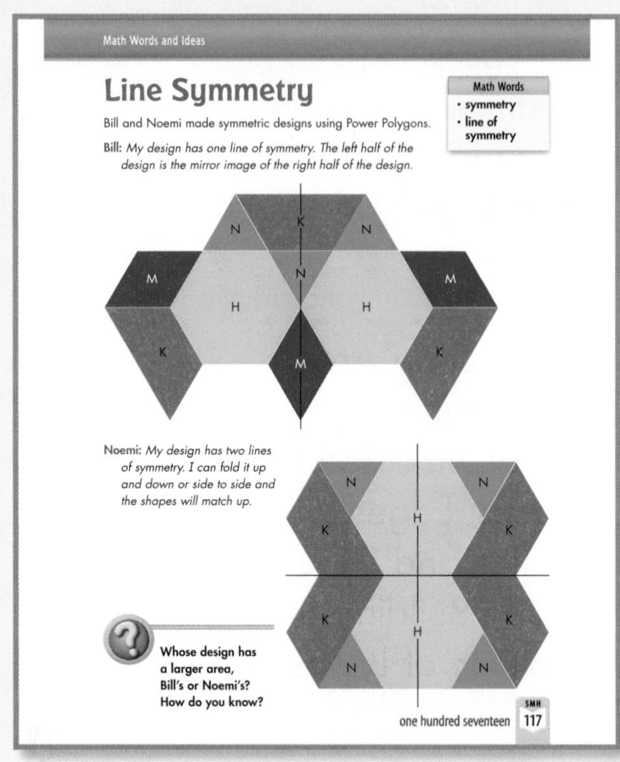

Math Words and Ideas

Line Symmetry

Math Words
- symmetry
- line of symmetry

Bill and Noemi made symmetric designs using Power Polygons.

Bill: *My design has one line of symmetry. The left half of the design is the mirror image of the right half of the design.*

Noemi: *My design has two lines of symmetry. I can fold it up and down or side to side and the shapes will match up.*

Whose design has a larger area, Bill's or Noemi's? How do you know?

one hundred seventeen SMH 117

▲ Student Math Handbook, p. 117

Games

You can use the Games pages to go over game rules during class or at home. They also list the materials and recording sheets needed to play each game.

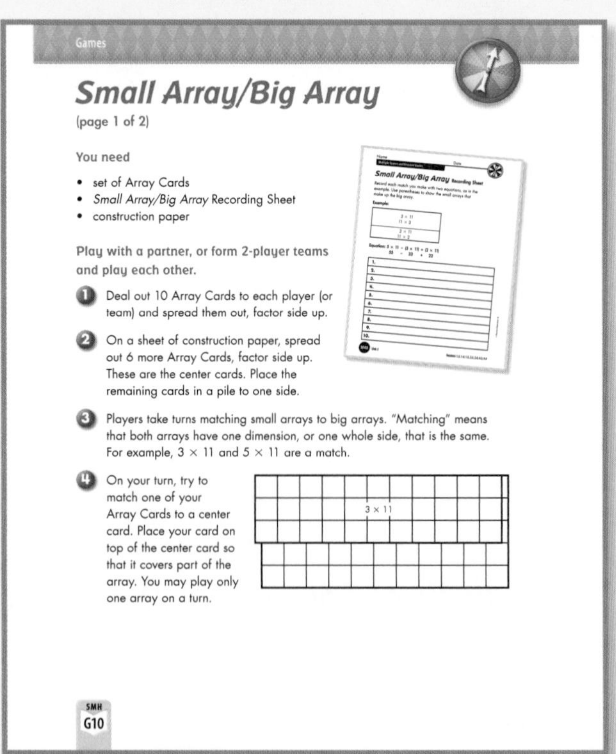

Games

Small Array/Big Array

(page 1 of 2)

You need

- set of Array Cards
- *Small Array/Big Array* Recording Sheet
- construction paper

Play with a partner, or form 2-player teams and play each other.

1. Deal out 10 Array Cards to each player (or team) and spread them out, factor side up.
2. On a sheet of construction paper, spread out 6 more Array Cards, factor side up. These are the center cards. Place the remaining cards in a pile to one side.
3. Players take turns matching small arrays to big arrays. "Matching" means that both arrays have one dimension, or one whole side, that is the same. For example, 3×11 and 5×11 are a match.
4. On your turn, try to match one of your Array Cards to a center card. Place your card on top of the center card so that it covers part of the array. You may play only one array on a turn.

SMH G10

▲ Student Math Handbook, p. G10

Daily Practice and **Homework** pages list useful *Student Math Handbook* (SMH) pages.

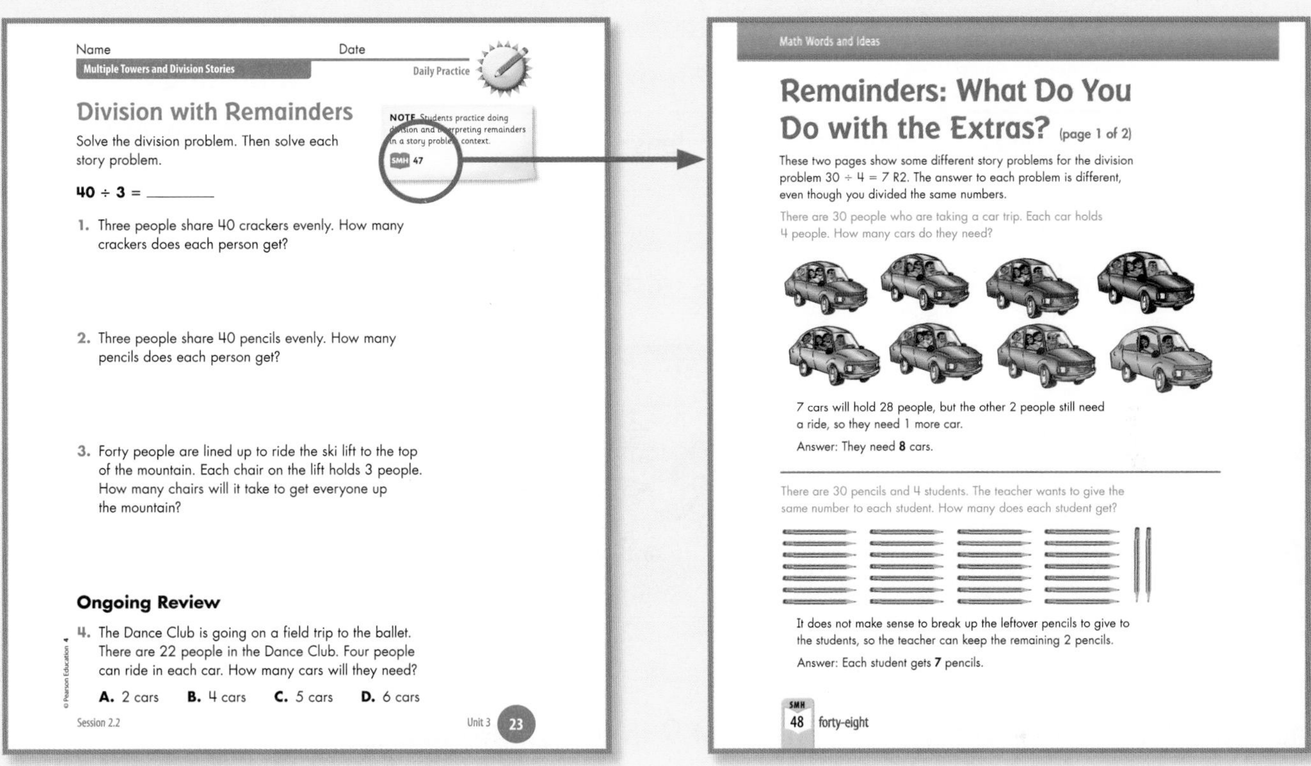

Name Date

Multiple Towers and Division Stories — Daily Practice

Division with Remainders

Solve the division problem. Then solve each story problem.

NOTE Students practice doing division and interpreting remainders in a story problem context.

SMH 47

40 ÷ 3 = ________

1. Three people share 40 crackers evenly. How many crackers does each person get?

2. Three people share 40 pencils evenly. How many pencils does each person get?

3. Forty people are lined up to ride the ski lift to the top of the mountain. Each chair on the lift holds 3 people. How many chairs will it take to get everyone up the mountain?

Ongoing Review

4. The Dance Club is going on a field trip to the ballet. There are 22 people in the Dance Club. Four people can ride in each car. How many cars will they need?

A. 2 cars **B.** 4 cars **C.** 5 cars **D.** 6 cars

© Pearson Education 4

Session 2.2 Unit 3 23

Math Words and Ideas

Remainders: What Do You Do with the Extras? (page 1 of 2)

These two pages show some different story problems for the division problem 30 ÷ 4 = 7 R2. The answer to each problem is different, even though you divided the same numbers.

There are 30 people who are taking a car trip. Each car holds 4 people. How many cars do they need?

7 cars will hold 28 people, but the other 2 people still need a ride, so they need 1 more car.

Answer: They need **8** cars.

There are 30 pencils and 4 students. The teacher wants to give the same number to each student. How many does each student get?

It does not make sense to break up the leftover pencils to give to the students, so the teacher can keep the remaining 2 pencils.

Answer: Each student gets **7** pencils.

SMH 48 forty-eight

▲ Student Activity Book, Unit 3, p. 23

▲ Student Math Handbook, pp. 48–49

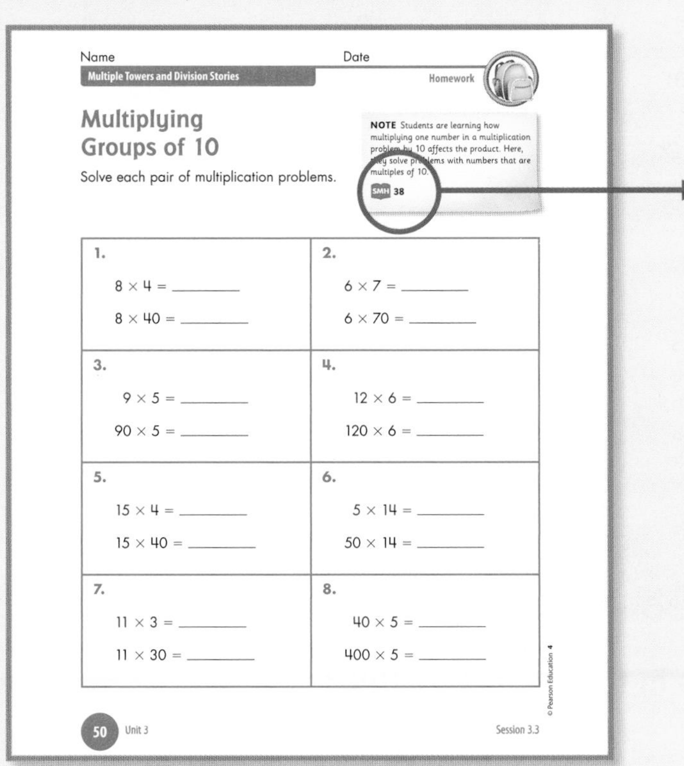

Name Date

Multiple Towers and Division Stories — Homework

Multiplying Groups of 10

Solve each pair of multiplication problems.

NOTE Students are learning how multiplying one number in a multiplication problem by 10 affects the product. Here, they solve problems with numbers that are multiples of 10.

SMH 38

1. 8 × 4 = ____ 8 × 40 = ____	2. 6 × 7 = ____ 6 × 70 = ____
3. 9 × 5 = ____ 90 × 5 = ____	4. 12 × 6 = ____ 120 × 6 = ____
5. 15 × 4 = ____ 15 × 40 = ____	6. 5 × 14 = ____ 50 × 14 = ____
7. 11 × 3 = ____ 11 × 30 = ____	8. 40 × 5 = ____ 400 × 5 = ____

© Pearson Education 4

50 Unit 3 Session 3.3

▲ Student Activity Book, Unit 3, p. 50

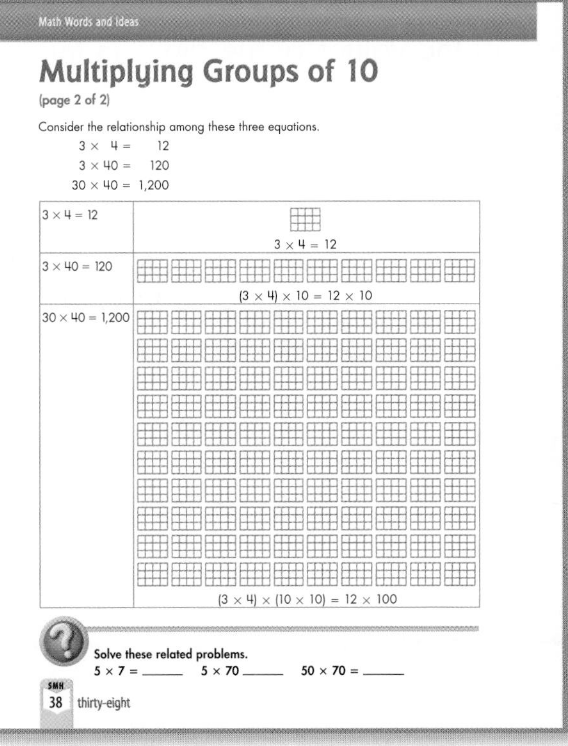

Math Words and Ideas

Multiplying Groups of 10

(page 2 of 2)

Consider the relationship among these three equations.

3 × 4 = 12
3 × 40 = 120
30 × 40 = 1,200

3 × 4 = 12	3 × 4 = 12
3 × 40 = 120	(3 × 4) × 10 = 12 × 10
30 × 40 = 1,200	(3 × 4) × (10 × 10) = 12 × 100

Solve these related problems.

5 × 7 = ____ 5 × 70 ____ 50 × 70 = ____

SMH 38 thirty-eight

▲ Student Math Handbook, p. 38

Place Value

The value of a digit changes depending on its place in a number.

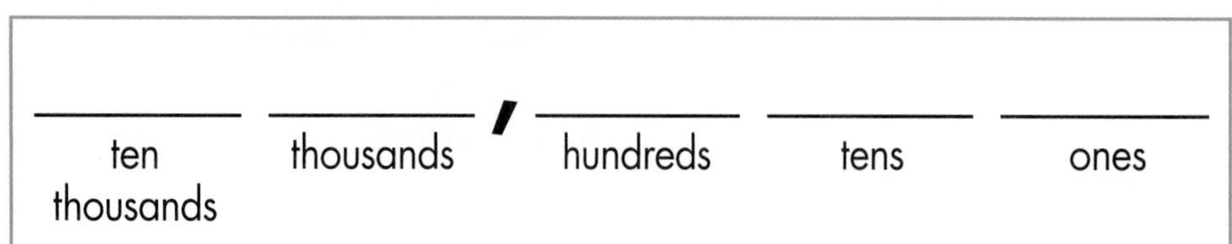

Math Words
- **place value**
- **ones**
- **tens**
- **hundreds**
- **thousands**
- **ten thousands**
- **digit**

In the two examples below, the digit 9 has different values.

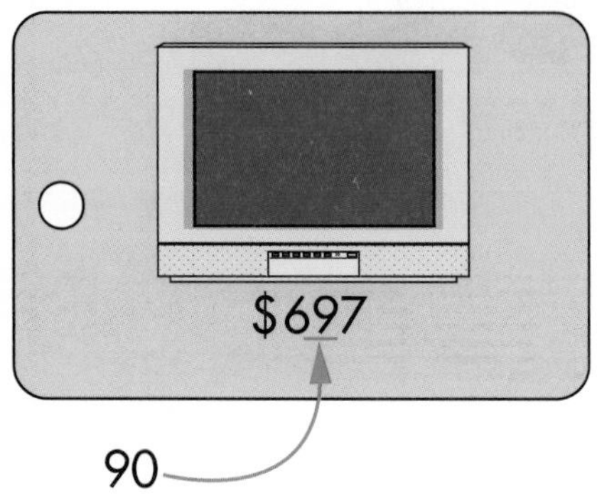

90

The digit 9 in the tens place represents 90.

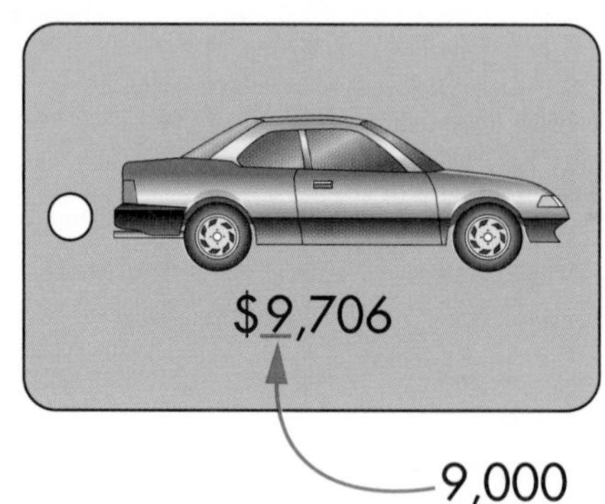

9,000

The digit 9 in the thousands place represents 9,000.

Look at the values of the digits in this number.

12,706 (twelve thousand, seven hundred six)
the digit 1 represents 10,000
the digit 2 represents 2,000
the digit 7 represents 700
the digit 0 represents 0 tens
the digit 6 represents 6

12,706 = 10,000 + 2,000 + 700 + 6

What are the values of the digits in the number 13,048?

Place Value of Large Numbers

Math Words
- **million**
- **billion**
- **trillion**
- **googol**

We name very large numbers by using a pattern.

TRILLIONS			BILLIONS			MILLIONS			THOUSANDS			ONES		
___	___	___,	___	___	___,	___	___	___,	___	___	___,	___	___	___
hundred trillions	ten trillions	one trillions	hundred billions	ten billions	one billions	hundred millions	ten millions	one millions	hundred thousands	ten thousands	one thousands	hundreds	tens	ones

Every three digits are separated by a comma.
The three grouped digits share a name (such as "millions").

Within a group of three digits, there is a pattern of ones, tens, and hundreds.

Very large numbers are used to count heartbeats.

(one)	about 1	heartbeat per second
(one thousand)	1,000	heartbeats in less than 20 minutes
(one million)	1,000,000	heartbeats in less than 2 weeks
(one billion)	1,000,000,000	heartbeats in about 35 years

A googol is a very, very large number!
One googol is written with the digit 1 followed by 100 zeros:

10,000,000,000,000,000,000,000,000,000,000,000,000,000,000,
000,000,000,000,000,000,000,000,000,000,000,000,000,000,000,
000,000,000,000,000,000

Addition Strategies

(page 1 of 2)

In Grade 4, you are using different strategies to solve addition problems efficiently. Here is an example:

$$\begin{array}{r} 1{,}852 \\ +\ 688 \\ \hline \end{array}$$

Breaking the Numbers Apart

Cheyenne solved this problem by adding one number in parts.

Cheyenne's solution

1,852 + 688 =

1,852 + 600 = 2,452

2,452 + 80 = 2,532

2,532 + 8 = **2,540**

Richard and Jill solved the problem by adding by place. Their solutions are similar, but they recorded their work differently.

Richard's solution

1,852 + 688 =	
1,800 + 600 =	2,400
50 + 80 =	130
2 + 8 =	10
	2,540

Jill's solution

$$\begin{array}{r} 1{,}852 \\ +\ 688 \\ \hline 1{,}000 \\ 1{,}400 \\ 130 \\ +\ 10 \\ \hline \mathbf{2{,}540} \end{array}$$

Addition Strategies

(page 2 of 2)

$$\begin{array}{r} 1{,}852 \\ +\ 688 \\ \hline \end{array}$$

Changing the Numbers

Emaan solved the problem by changing one number and adjusting the sum. He changed 688 to 700 to make an easier problem to solve.

Emaan's solution

$$\begin{array}{r} 1{,}852 \\ +\ 700 \\ \hline 2{,}552 \\ -\ 12 \\ \hline \mathbf{2{,}540} \end{array}$$

I added 700 instead of 688.

Then I subtracted the extra 12.

Venetta solved this problem by creating an equivalent problem.

Venetta's solution

1,852 + 688 =

(−12) (+12) *I added 12 to 688 and subtracted 12 from 1,852.*

1,840 + 700 = **2,540**

Show how you would solve the problem 1,852 + 688.

Comparing Addition Notation

$564 + 278 =$

Jake and Anna solved this problem by adding by place. Their solutions are similar, but they recorded their work differently.

Jake's solution

```
  564
+ 278
-----
  700
  130
   12
-----
  842
```

Anna's solution (U.S. Algorithm)

```
  1 1
  564
+ 278
-----
  842
```

The students in Jake and Anna's class compared the notation used in these two solutions. Here are some of the things they noticed:

Both solutions involve breaking numbers apart by place.
Jake added the hundreds first, then the tens, and then the ones.
Anna added the ones first, then the tens, and then the hundreds.

The little numbers in the U.S. algorithm stand for 10s and 100s.

The strategies are mostly the same, but the U.S. algorithm notation combines steps.

The last step in Jake's solution is the same as the first step in Anna's solution: $4 + 8 = 12$.

In the U.S. algorithm you "carry" 10 ones to the tens place, and you "carry" 10 tens to the hundreds place.

Subtraction Situations

(page 1 of 2)

Finding the Missing Part

Lucy's family visited their grandparents, who live 572 miles from their house. On the first day they drove 389 miles. How many miles do they have left to drive on the second day?

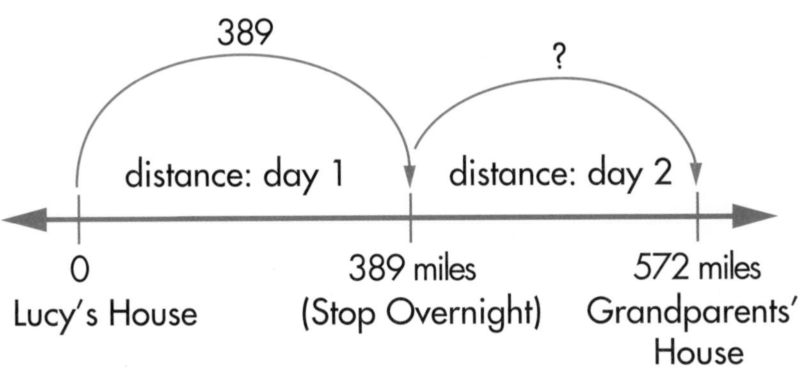

Comparing Two Amounts

The Bankhead School has 436 girls and 378 boys. How many more girls than boys are there at the school?

436 Girls	
378 Boys	?

Subtraction Situations

(page 2 of 2)

Removing an Amount

Helena had $8.56. She spent $4.35 on a gift for her mother. How much money does Helena have left?

Dollars

Dimes

Pennies

Subtraction Strategies

(page 1 of 3)

In Grade 4, you are using different strategies to solve subtraction problems efficiently. Here is an example:

$$\begin{array}{r} 924 \\ -\ 672 \\ \hline \end{array}$$

Subtracting in Parts

Amelia solved this problem by subtracting in parts.

Amelia's solution

924 − 672 =

924 − 600 = 324
324 − 20 = 304
304 − 50 = 254
254 − 2 = **252**

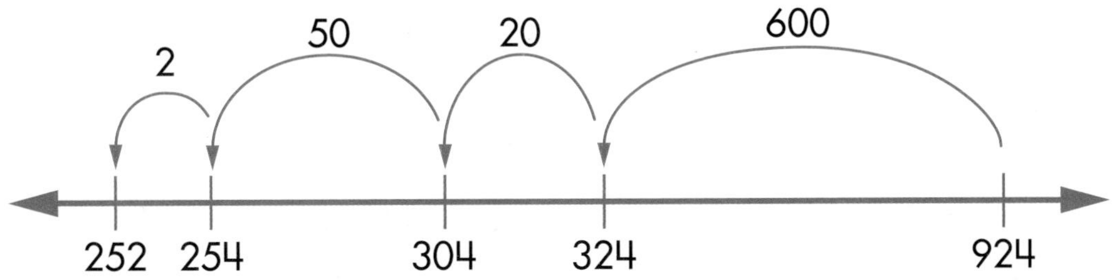

I started at 924, and jumped back 672 in four parts (−600, −20, −50, −2).

I landed on 252.

The answer is the place where I landed.

924 − 672 = **252**

Subtraction Strategies

(page 2 of 3)

$$\begin{array}{r} 924 \\ -\ 672 \\ \hline \end{array}$$

Adding Up

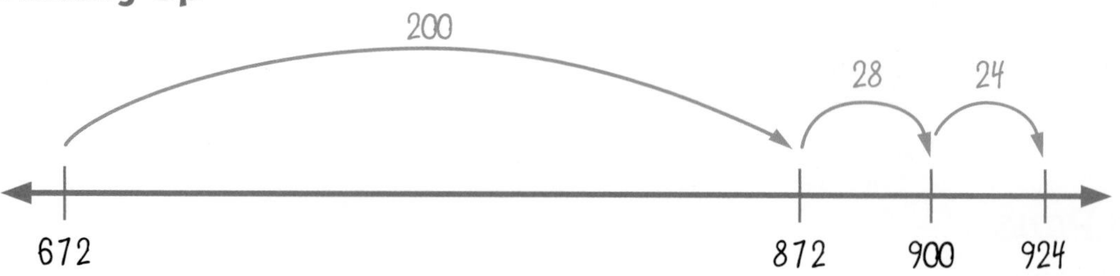

Jake used an adding-up strategy to solve 924 − 672.

Jake's solution

672 + ___?___ = 924

672 + ___200___ = 872

872 + ___28___ = 900

900 + ___24___ = 924

200 + 28 + 24 = **252** *The answer is the total of all of the jumps from 672 up to 924.*

Subtracting Back

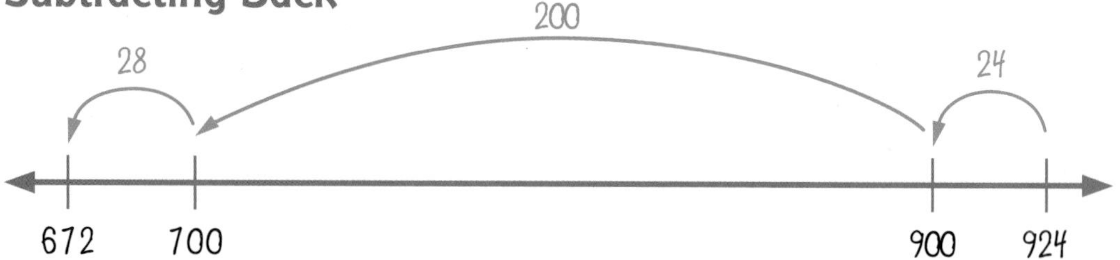

Luke used a subtracting-back strategy.

Luke's solution

924 − ___24___ = 900

900 − ___200___ = 700

700 − ___28___ = 672

24 + 200 + 28 = **252** *The answer is the total of all the jumps from 924 back to 672.*

Subtraction Strategies

(page 3 of 3)

$$\begin{array}{r} 924 \\ -\ 672 \\ \hline \end{array}$$

Changing the Numbers

Sabrina and Ursula solved 924 − 672 by changing the numbers to make an easier problem to solve.

Sabrina's solution

Sabrina changed one number and then adjusted to find her answer.

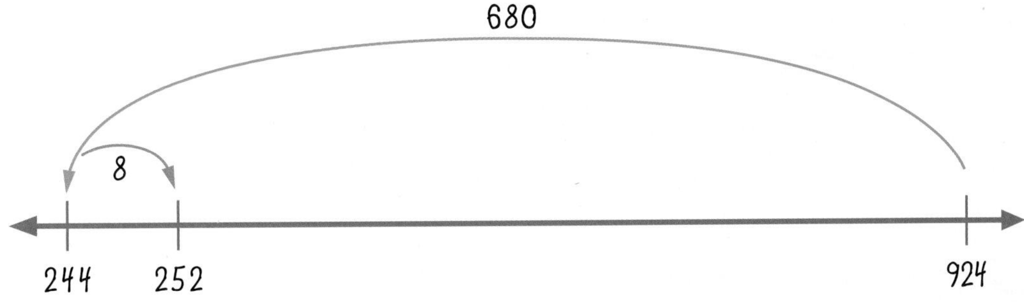

924 − 672 =

924 - 680 = 244 *I subtracted 680 instead of 672.*

244 + 8 = **252** *I subtracted too much, so I have to add 8 back on.*

Ursula's solution

Ursula solved this problem by creating an equivalent problem.

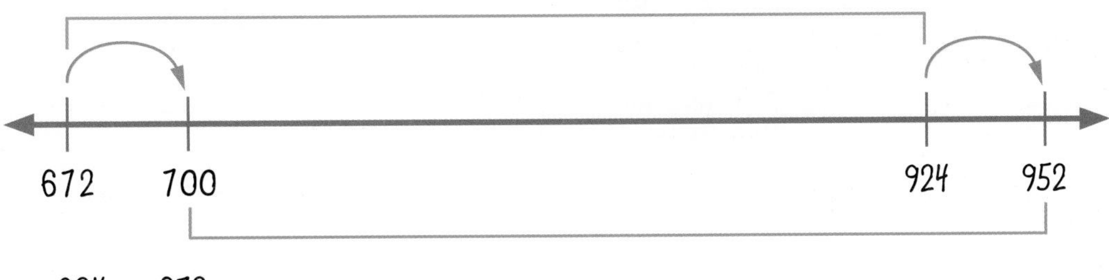

924 - 672 =

(+28) (+28)

952 - 700 = **252**

Show how you would solve the problem 924 − 672.

Multiplication (page 1 of 2)

Math Words
- **multiplication**
- **factor**
- **product**

Use multiplication when you want to combine groups that are the same size.

How many oranges are in this box?

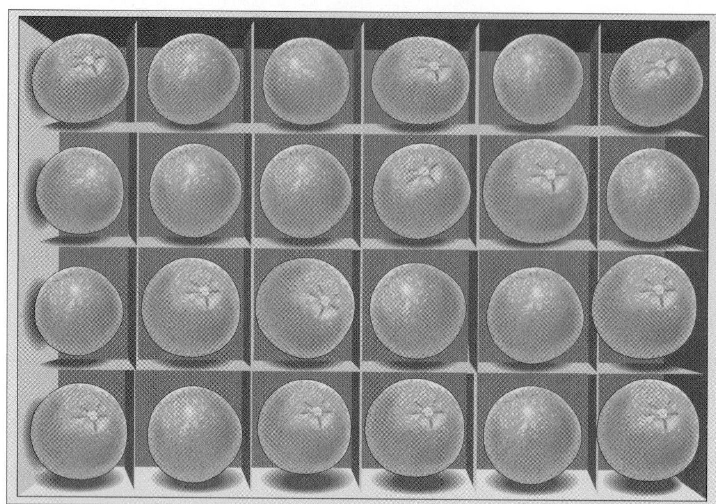

There are 4 rows of oranges.
There are 6 oranges in each row.
There are 24 oranges in the box.

$4 \times 6 = 24$

4 and 6: factors; 24: product

$$\begin{array}{r} 4 \\ \times\ 6 \\ \hline 24 \end{array}$$

4 and 6: factors; 24: product

Multiplication (page 2 of 2)

Here is an example of multiplication with larger numbers.

The audience at the school play filled up 6 rows in the auditorium. Each row had 15 seats. How many people were in the audience?

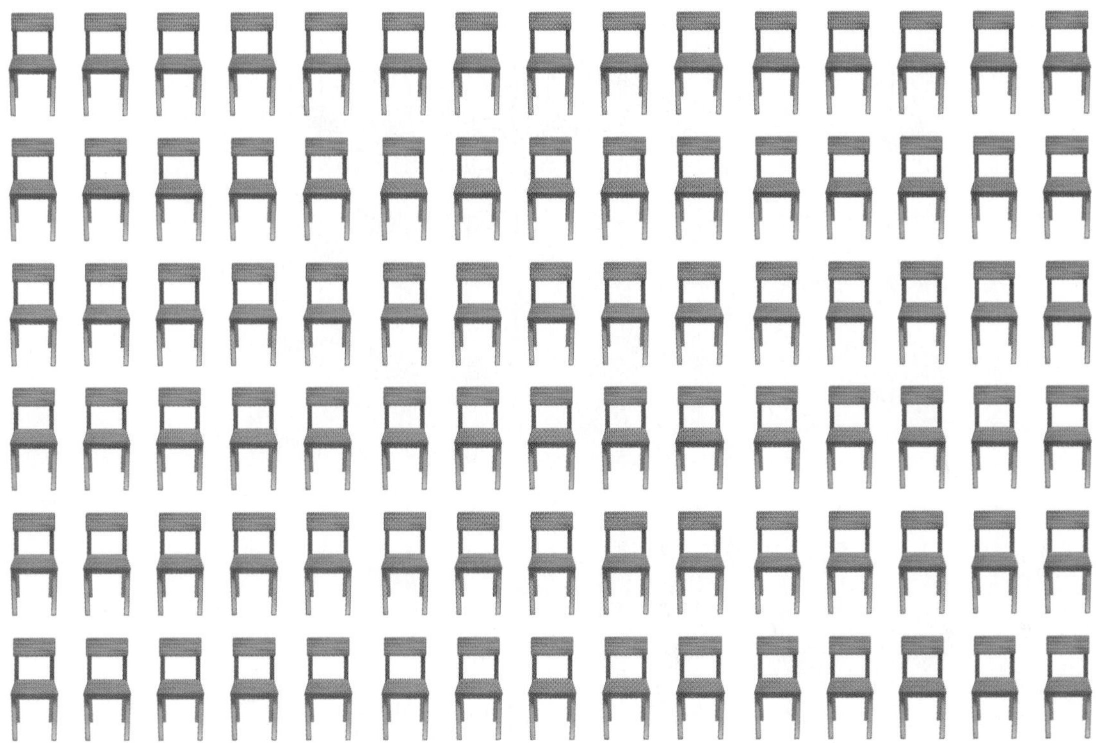

There are 6 rows.
Each row has 15 people.
There are 90 people in the audience.

$6 \times 15 = 90$

6 and 15 are factors; 90 is the product.

$$\begin{array}{r} 6 \\ \times\ 15 \\ \hline 90 \end{array}$$

6 and 15 are factors; 90 is the product.

What are the factors in 8 × 5 = 40? What is the product?

Arrays (page 1 of 2)

Math Words
- **array**
- **dimension**

An array is one way to represent multiplication.

Here is an array of chairs.

There are 5 rows of chairs.

There are 9 chairs in each row.

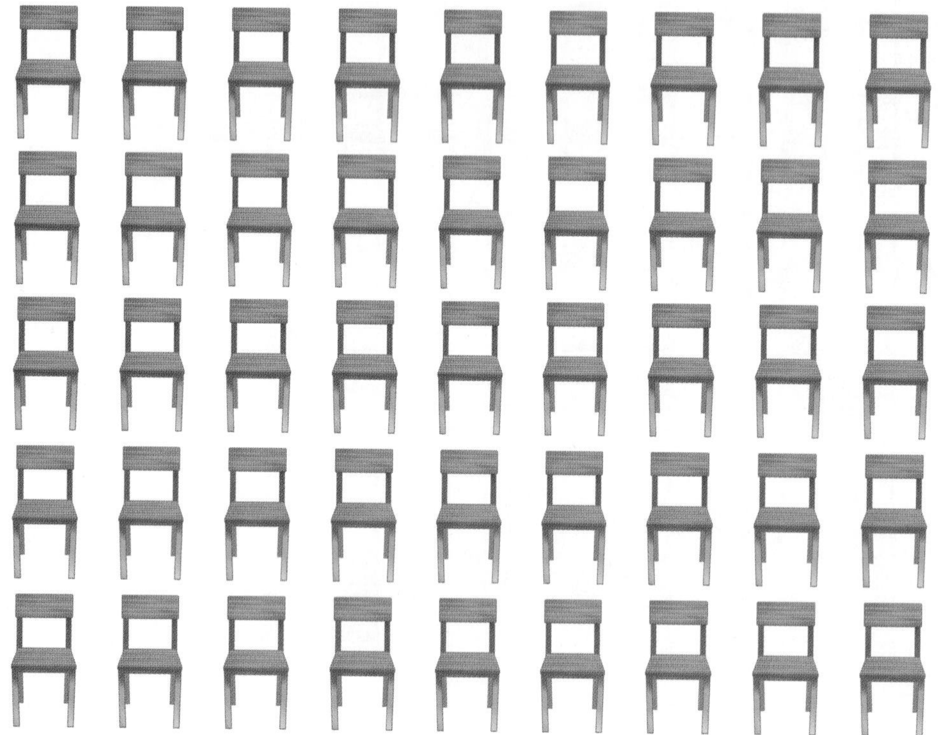

The arrangement of chairs can be represented as a rectangle.

When we talk about the size of an array, we say that the dimensions are "5 by 9" (or "9 by 5," depending on how you are looking at the array).

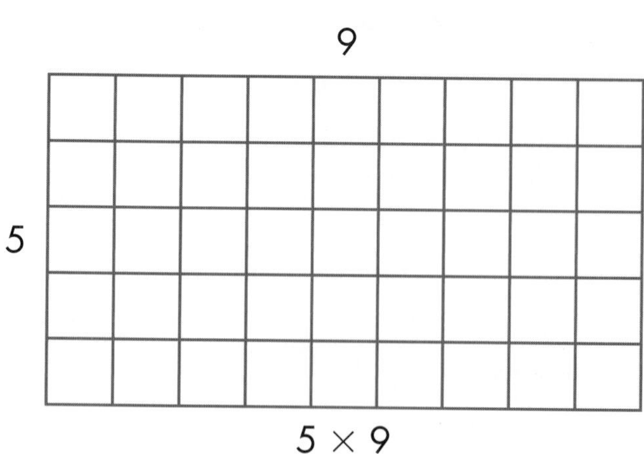

5×9

What are the dimensions of this array?

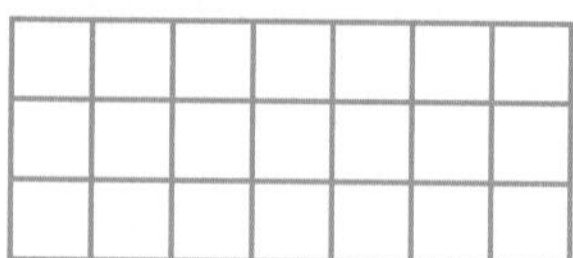

Arrays (page 2 of 2)

Here are some examples of rectangular arrays that show how multiplication problems can be broken into smaller parts.

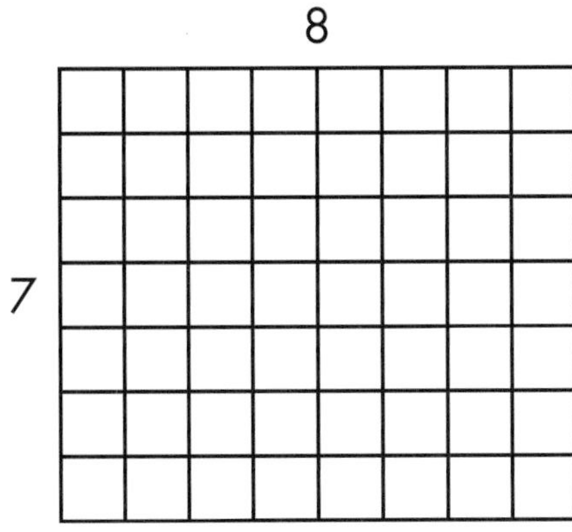

This 7 by 8 array can be broken into parts to find the product in many different ways.

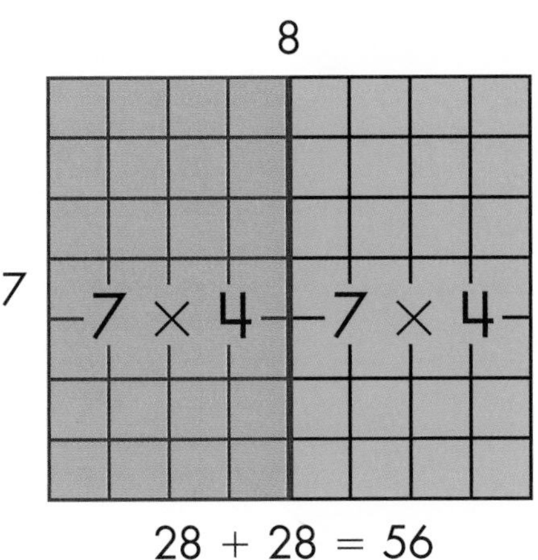

28 + 28 = 56

8

7

7 × 5

7 × 3

35 + 21 = 56

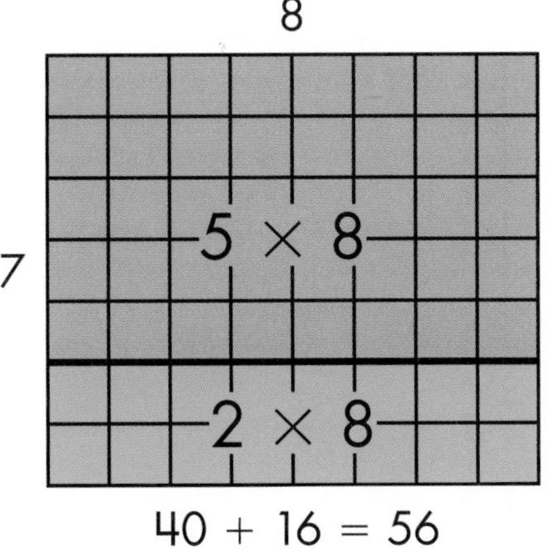

40 + 16 = 56

8

7

4 × 8

3 × 8

32 + 24 = 56

All of these arrays show that the product of 7 × 8 is 56.

Unmarked Arrays (page 1 of 2)

With larger numbers, unmarked arrays can be easier to use than arrays with grid lines. You can imagine the rows of squares without drawing them all.

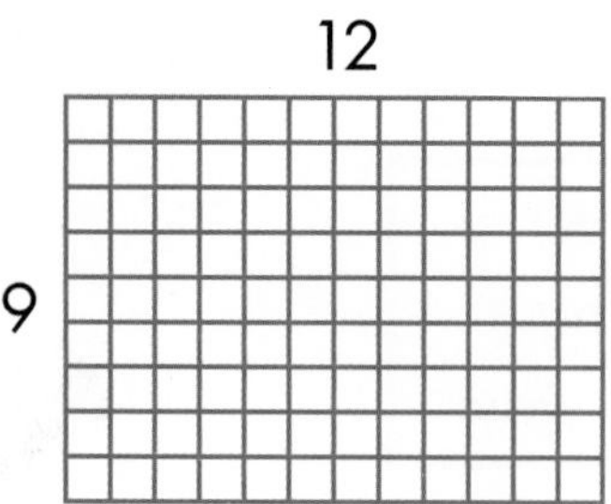

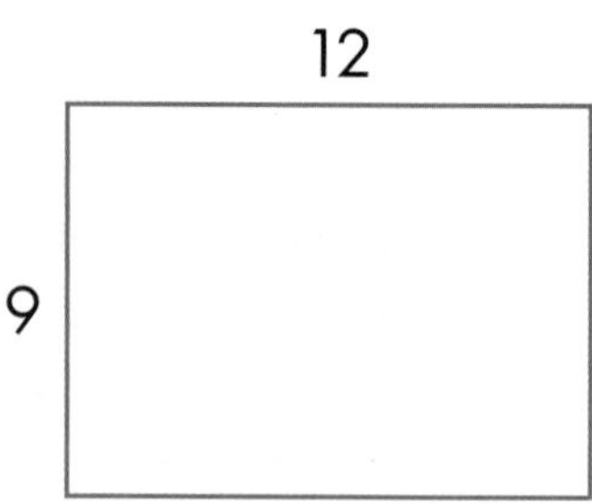

Look at the ways that unmarked arrays are used to show different ways to solve the problem 9×12.

12

9: 3 | $3 \times 12 = 36$
3 | $3 \times 12 = 36$
3 | $3 \times 12 = 36$

$9 \times 12 = (3 \times 12) + (3 \times 12) + (3 \times 12)$
$9 \times 12 = 36 + 36 + 36$
$9 \times 12 =$ **108**

12

6 | 6

9: $9 \times 6 = 54$ | $9 \times 6 = 54$

$9 \times 12 = (9 \times 6) + (9 \times 6)$
$9 \times 12 = 54 + 54$
$9 \times 12 =$ **108**

12

10 | 2

9: $9 \times 10 = 90$ | $9 \times 2 = 18$

$9 \times 12 = (9 \times 10) + (9 \times 2)$
$9 \times 12 = 90 + 18$
$9 \times 12 =$ **108**

Unmarked Arrays (page 2 of 2)

These unmarked arrays show different ways to solve the problem 14 × 20.

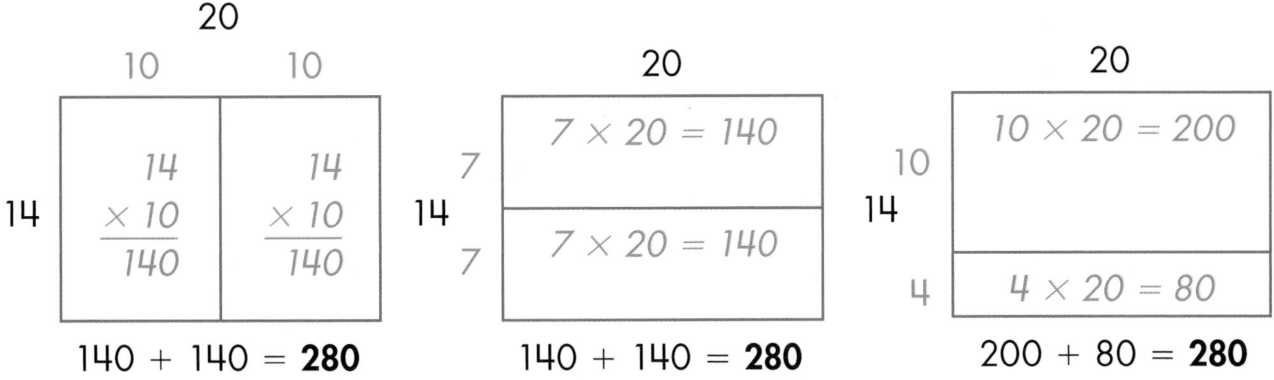

This unmarked array shows a solution for 34 × 45.

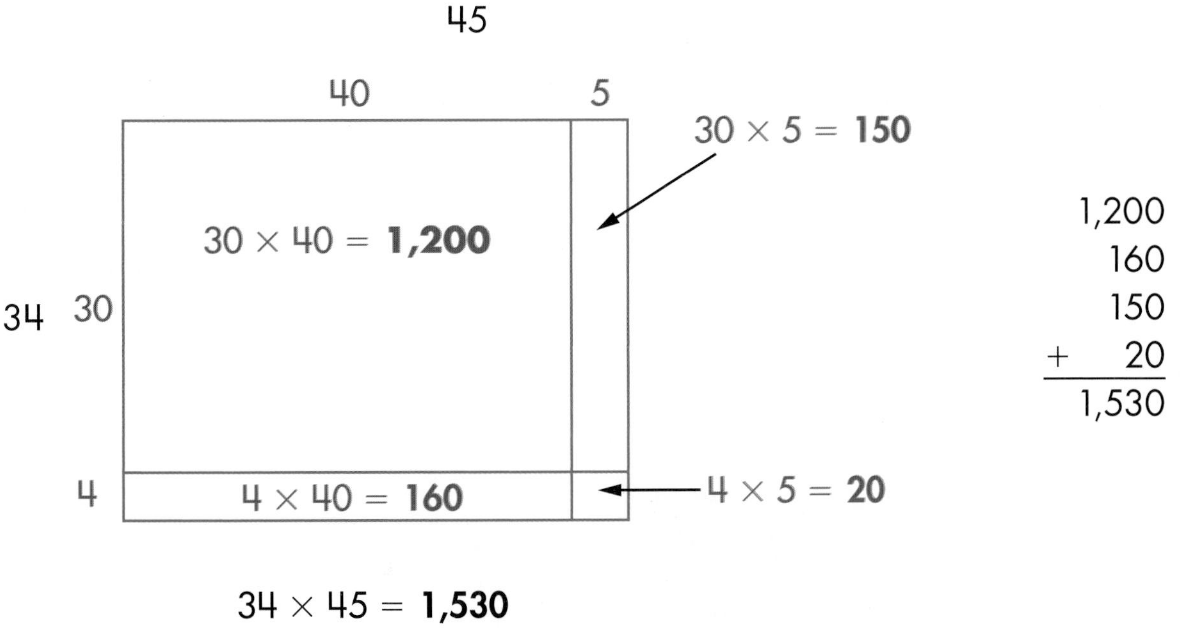

Use unmarked arrays to show some ways to solve 8 × 14.

Factors

These three students have different ways to think about factors and different ways to show that 4 is a factor of 32.

Bill: *A factor is a whole number that divides another number evenly, with nothing left over.*

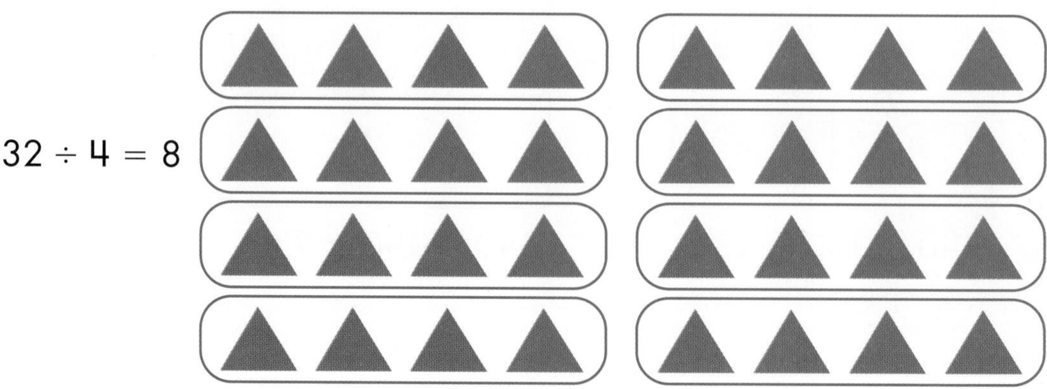

So I know that 4 is a factor of 32.

Sabrina: *A factor is one of the dimensions of a rectangular array.*

There are 32 tiles here in a 4-by-8 array.

So I know that 4 is a factor of 32.

(And 8 is a factor of 32, too!)

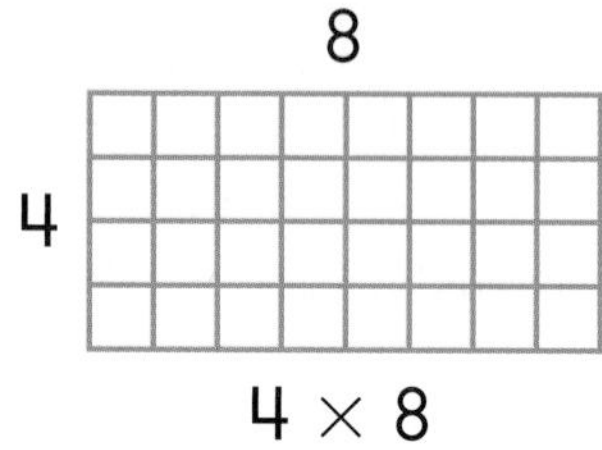

Derek: *You can skip count by a factor of a number and land exactly on that number.*

I can skip count by 4s to get to 32.
4, 8, 12, 16, 20, 24, 28, 32!

So I know that 4 is a factor of 32.

What are some other factors of 32?

Factors of 24

These are all the possible rectangular arrays that can be made with 24 square tiles.

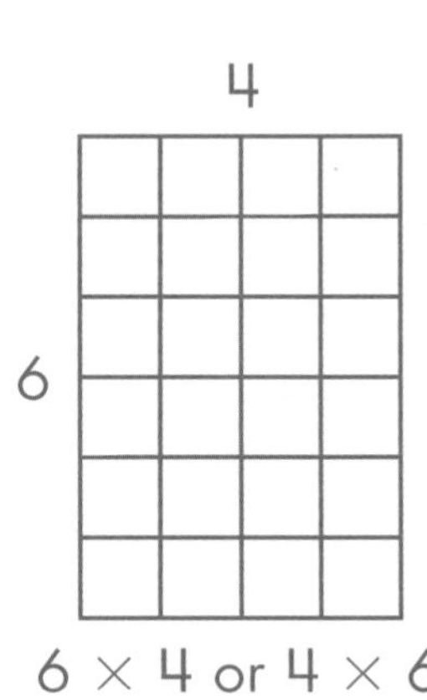

6×4 or 4×6

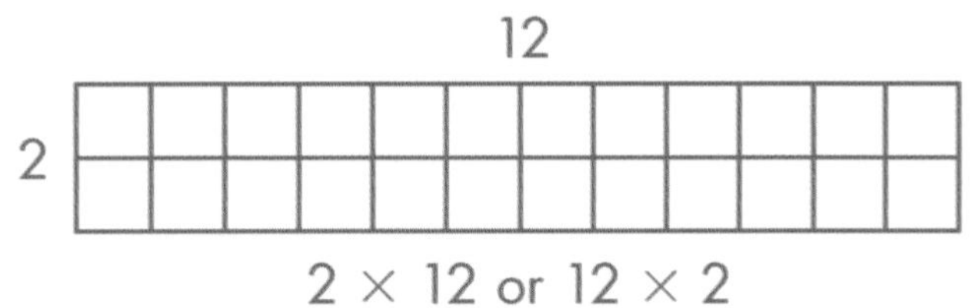

2×12 or 12×2

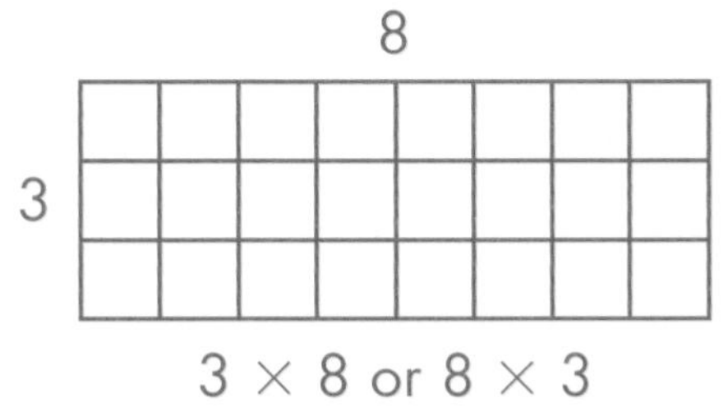

3×8 or 8×3

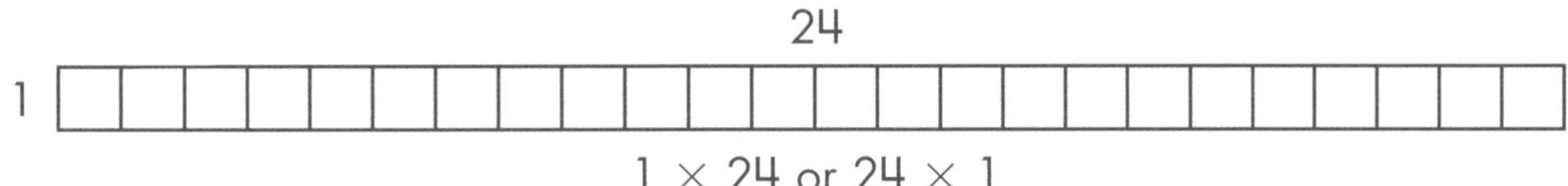

1×24 or 24×1

Each dimension of these rectangles is a factor of 24.

Listed in order, the factors of 24 are:

1 2 3 4 6 8 12 24

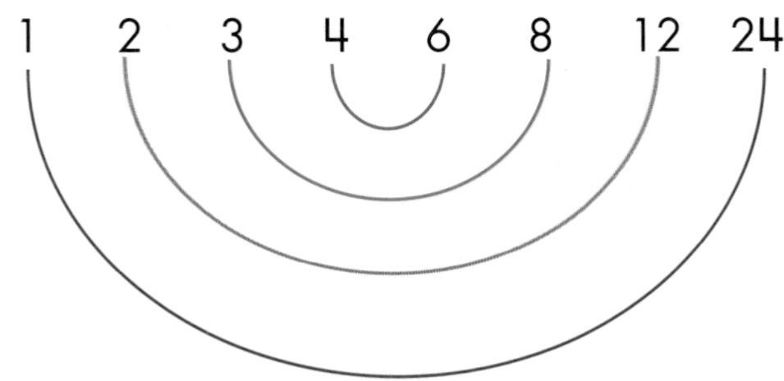

Pairs of factors can be multiplied to get a product of 24.

$1 \times 24 = 24$	$2 \times 12 = 24$	$3 \times 8 = 24$	$4 \times 6 = 24$
$24 \times 1 = 24$	$12 \times 2 = 24$	$8 \times 3 = 24$	$6 \times 4 = 24$

Multiples

Math Words
- **multiples**

This 100 chart shows skip counting by 8.

The shaded numbers are multiples of 8.

1	2	3	4	5	6	7	8	9	10
11	12	13	14	15	16	17	18	19	20
21	22	23	24	25	26	27	28	29	30
31	32	33	34	35	36	37	38	39	40
41	42	43	44	45	46	47	48	49	50
51	52	53	54	55	56	57	58	59	60
61	62	63	64	65	66	67	68	69	70
71	72	73	74	75	76	77	78	79	80
81	82	83	84	85	86	87	88	89	90
91	92	93	94	95	96	97	98	99	100

8	1×8
16	2×8
24	3×8
32	4×8
40	5×8
48	6×8
56	7×8
64	8×8
72	9×8
80	10×8
88	11×8
96	12×8

A store sells CDs for $8 each.

1 CD costs $8.

2 CDs cost $16.

3 CDs cost $24.

4 CDs cost $32.

The prices for buying CDs are multiples of 8:
$8, $16, $24, $32, …

How could you use multiples to find the price of 7 CDs?

Multiples: Counting Around the Class

Mr. Field's class counted by 15s. The first person said 15, the second person said 30, the third said 45, and so on. The last person said 300.

The numbers they shaded on this 300 chart are multiples of 15.

1	2	3	4	5	6	7	8	9	10
11	12	13	14	15	16	17	18	19	20
21	22	23	24	25	26	27	28	29	30
31	32	33	34	35	36	37	38	39	40
41	42	43	44	45	46	47	48	49	50
51	52	53	54	55	56	57	58	59	60
61	62	63	64	65	66	67	68	69	70
71	72	73	74	75	76	77	78	79	80
81	82	83	84	85	86	87	88	89	90
91	92	93	94	95	96	97	98	99	100
101	102	103	104	105	106	107	108	109	110
111	112	113	114	115	116	117	118	119	120
121	122	123	124	125	126	127	128	129	130
131	132	133	134	135	136	137	138	139	140
141	142	143	144	145	146	147	148	149	150
151	152	153	154	155	156	157	158	159	160
161	162	163	164	165	166	167	168	169	170
171	172	173	174	175	176	177	178	179	180
181	182	183	184	185	186	187	188	189	190
191	192	193	194	195	196	197	198	199	200
201	202	203	204	205	206	207	208	209	210
211	212	213	214	215	216	217	218	219	220
221	222	223	224	225	226	227	228	229	230
231	232	233	234	235	236	237	238	239	240
241	242	243	244	245	246	247	248	249	250
251	252	253	254	255	256	257	258	259	260
261	262	263	264	265	266	267	268	269	270
271	272	273	274	275	276	277	278	279	280
281	282	283	284	285	286	287	288	289	290
291	292	293	294	295	296	297	298	299	300

15
30
45
60
75
90
105
120
135
150
165
.
.
.

☐ × **15** = 300

300 ÷ **15** = ☐

How many people counted to get to 300?
How do you know?

Factors and Multiples

Consider this list of equations:

$$4 \times 4 = 16$$
$$5 \times 4 = 20$$
$$6 \times 4 = 24$$
$$7 \times 4 = 28$$
$$8 \times 4 = 32$$
$$9 \times 4 = 36$$

4 is a factor of
16, 20, 24, 28, 32, 36,...

4 is a factor of any whole number that it divides evenly.

16, 20, 24, 28, 32, and 36 are some of the multiples of 4.

Multiply 4 by any number to get a multiple of 4.

Arrays can be used to picture factors and multiples.

32 is a multiple of 4, and 4 is a factor of 32. You can use exactly 32 tiles to make a rectangle with one dimension of 4.

30 is *not* a multiple of 4, and 4 is *not* a factor of 30. You cannot use exactly 30 tiles to make a rectangle with one dimension of 4.

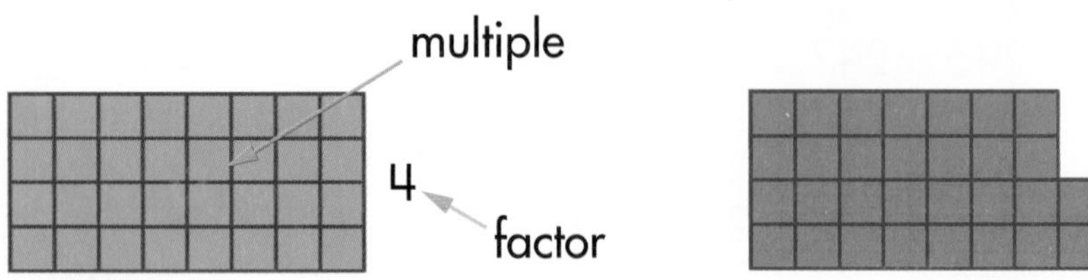

Is 4 a factor of 48? Is 21 a multiple of 4?

Prime Numbers

Math Words
- **prime number**
- **composite number**

Prime numbers have exactly two factors, 1 and the number itself.

23 is a prime number. The only factors of 23 are 1 and 23. There is only one rectangle that can be made with 23 tiles.

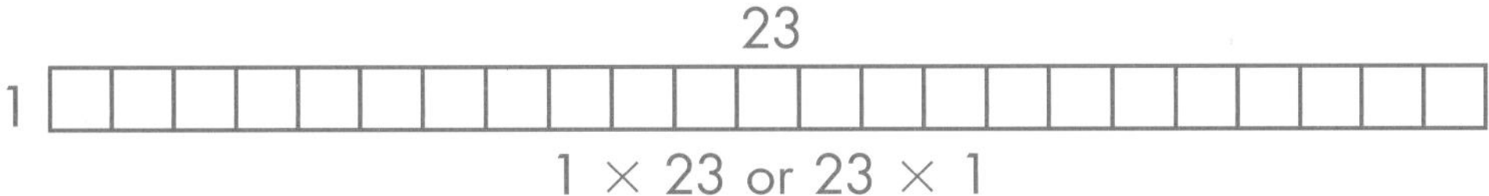

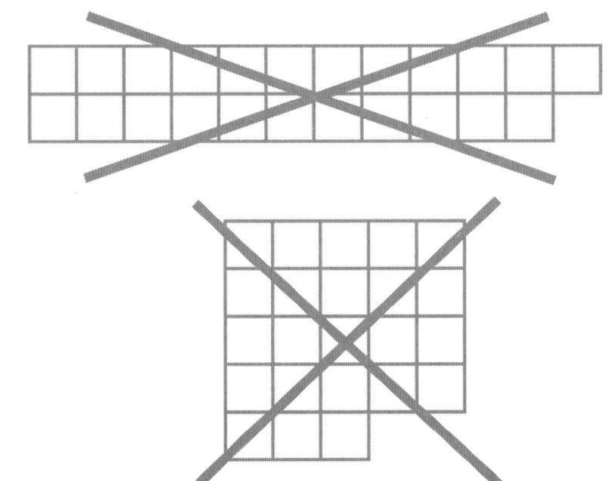

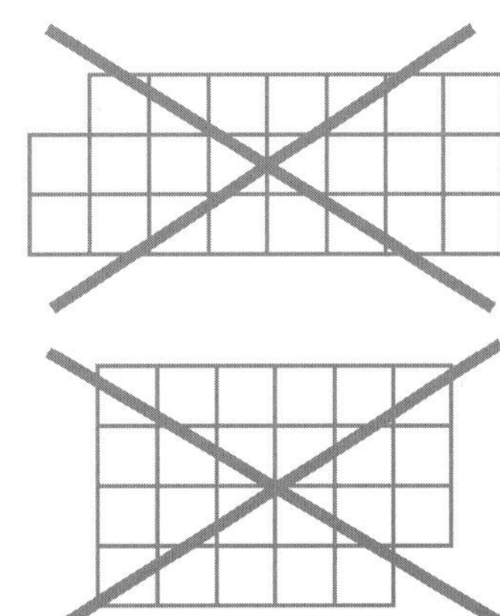

Numbers that have more than 2 factors are called composite numbers.

12 is a composite number. There are several pairs of whole numbers that can be multiplied to equal 12.

$1 \times 12 = 12$
$2 \times 6 = 12$
$3 \times 4 = 12$
$4 \times 3 = 12$
$6 \times 2 = 12$
$12 \times 1 = 12$

The number 1 has only one factor. It is neither a prime number nor a composite number.

Find all the prime numbers up to 50.

Square Numbers

Math Words
- **square number**

A square number can be represented by a square array.
A square number is made when a number is multiplied by itself.

9 is a square number. 9 tiles can make a square array.

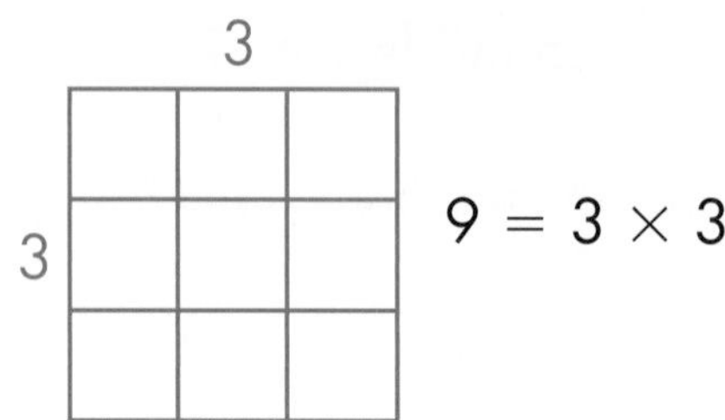

1, 4, 9, 16, and 25 are all square numbers.

$$\begin{array}{r} 1 \\ \times\ 1 \\ \hline 1 \end{array} \quad \begin{array}{r} 2 \\ \times\ 2 \\ \hline 4 \end{array} \quad \begin{array}{r} 3 \\ \times\ 3 \\ \hline 9 \end{array} \quad \begin{array}{r} 4 \\ \times\ 4 \\ \hline 16 \end{array} \quad \begin{array}{r} 5 \\ \times\ 5 \\ \hline 25 \end{array}$$

400 is a square number because 20 × 20 = 400.

List all the square numbers up to 100.

Multiplication Combinations (page 1 of 6)

One of your goals in math class this year is to learn all the multiplication combinations up to 12 × 12.

1 x 1	1 x 2	1 x 3	1 x 4	1 x 5	1 x 6	1 x 7	1 x 8	1 x 9	1 x 10	1 x 11	1 x 12
2 x 1	2 x 2	2 x 3	2 x 4	2 x 5	2 x 6	2 x 7	2 x 8	2 x 9	2 x 10	2 x 11	2 x 12
3 x 1	3 x 2	3 x 3	3 x 4	3 x 5	3 x 6	3 x 7	3 x 8	3 x 9	3 x 10	3 x 11	3 x 12
4 x 1	4 x 2	4 x 3	4 x 4	4 x 5	4 x 6	4 x 7	4 x 8	4 x 9	4 x 10	4 x 11	4 x 12
5 x 1	5 x 2	5 x 3	5 x 4	5 x 5	5 x 6	5 x 7	5 x 8	5 x 9	5 x 10	5 x 11	5 x 12
6 x 1	6 x 2	6 x 3	6 x 4	6 x 5	6 x 6	6 x 7	6 x 8	6 x 9	6 x 10	6 x 11	6 x 12
7 x 1	7 x 2	7 x 3	7 x 4	7 x 5	7 x 6	7 x 7	7 x 8	7 x 9	7 x 10	7 x 11	7 x 12
8 x 1	8 x 2	8 x 3	8 x 4	8 x 5	8 x 6	8 x 7	8 x 8	8 x 9	8 x 10	8 x 11	8 x 12
9 x 1	9 x 2	9 x 3	9 x 4	9 x 5	9 x 6	9 x 7	9 x 8	9 x 9	9 x 10	9 x 11	9 x 12
10 x 1	10 x 2	10 x 3	10 x 4	10 x 5	10 x 6	10 x 7	10 x 8	10 x 9	10 x 10	10 x 11	10 x 12
11 x 1	11 x 2	11 x 3	11 x 4	11 x 5	11 x 6	11 x 7	11 x 8	11 x 9	11 x 10	11 x 11	11 x 12
12 x 1	12 x 2	12 x 3	12 x 4	12 x 5	12 x 6	12 x 7	12 x 8	12 x 9	12 x 10	12 x 11	12 x 12

There are 144 multiplication combinations on this chart. You may think that learning all of them is a challenge. (Remember that last year you learned all of them up to a product of 50.) On the next few pages you will find some suggestions to help you learn the multiplication combinations.

As you practice these multiplication combinations, make two lists like those shown.

Combinations I Know	Combinations I'm Working On

Multiplication Combinations (page 2 of 6)

Learning two combinations at a time

To help you learn multiplication combinations, think about two combinations at a time, such as 8×3 and 3×8.

These two problems look different, but have the same answer.

3

8

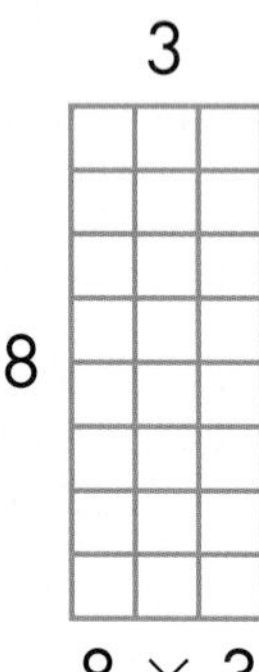

8×3

8

3

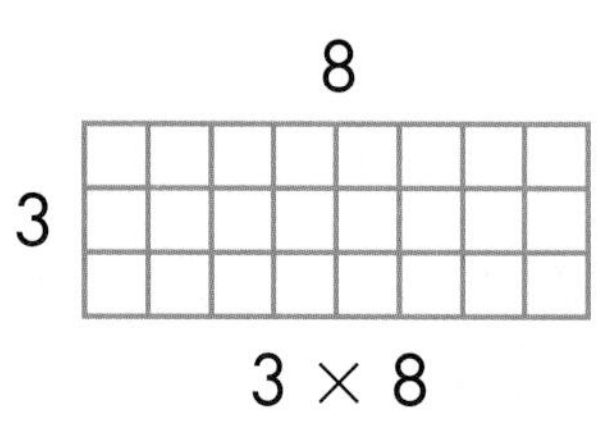

3×8

When you know that $8 \times 3 = 24$, you also know that $3 \times 8 = 24$.

You have learned two multiplication combinations!

By "turning around" combinations and learning them two at a time, the chart of multiplication combinations is reduced from 144 to 78 combinations to learn!

1 x 1	1 x 2	1 x 3	1 x 4	1 x 5	1 x 6	1 x 7	1 x 8	1 x 9	1 x 10	1 x 11	1 x 12
2 x 1 1 x 2	2 x 2	2 x 3	2 x 4	2 x 5	2 x 6	2 x 7	2 x 8	2 x 9	2 x 10	2 x 11	2 x 12
3 x 1 1 x 3	3 x 2 2 x 3	3 x 3	3 x 4	3 x 5	3 x 6	3 x 7	3 x 8	3 x 9	3 x 10	3 x 11	3 x 12
4 x 1 1 x 4	4 x 2 2 x 4	4 x 3 3 x 4	4 x 4	4 x 5	4 x 6	4 x 7	4 x 8	4 x 9	4 x 10	4 x 11	4 x 12
5 x 1 1 x 5	5 x 2 2 x 5	5 x 3 3 x 5	5 x 4 4 x 5	5 x 5	5 x 6	5 x 7	5 x 8	5 x 9	5 x 10	5 x 11	5 x 12
6 x 1 1 x 6	6 x 2 2 x 6	6 x 3 3 x 6	6 x 4 4 x 6	6 x 5 5 x 6	6 x 6	6 x 7	6 x 8	6 x 9	6 x 10	6 x 11	6 x 12
7 x 1 1 x 7	7 x 2 2 x 7	7 x 3 3 x 7	7 x 4 4 x 7	7 x 5 5 x 7	7 x 6 6 x 7	7 x 7	7 x 8	7 x 9	7 x 10	7 x 11	7 x 12
8 x 1 1 x 8	8 x 2 2 x 8	8 x 3 3 x 8	8 x 4 4 x 8	8 x 5 5 x 8	8 x 6 6 x 8	8 x 7 7 x 8	8 x 8	8 x 9	8 x 10	8 x 11	8 x 12
9 x 1 1 x 9	9 x 2 2 x 9	9 x 3 3 x 9	9 x 4 4 x 9	9 x 5 5 x 9	9 x 6 6 x 9	9 x 7 7 x 9	9 x 8 8 x 9	9 x 9	9 x 10	9 x 11	9 x 12
10 x 1 1 x 10	10 x 2 2 x 10	10 x 3 3 x 10	10 x 4 4 x 10	10 x 5 5 x 10	10 x 6 6 x 10	10 x 7 7 x 10	10 x 8 8 x 10	10 x 9 9 x 10	10 x 10	10 x 11	10 x 12
11 x 1 1 x 11	11 x 2 2 x 11	11 x 3 3 x 11	11 x 4 4 x 11	11 x 5 5 x 11	11 x 6 6 x 11	11 x 7 7 x 11	11 x 8 8 x 11	11 x 9 9 x 11	11 x 10 10 x 11	11 x 11	11 x 12
12 x 1 1 x 12	12 x 2 2 x 12	12 x 3 3 x 12	12 x 4 4 x 12	12 x 5 5 x 12	12 x 6 6 x 12	12 x 7 7 x 12	12 x 8 8 x 12	12 x 9 9 x 12	12 x 10 10 x 12	12 x 11 11 x 12	12 x 12

Multiplication Combinations (page 3 of 6)

A helpful way to learn multiplication combinations is to think about one category at a time. Here are some categories you may have seen before. You probably already know many of these combinations.

Learning the ×1 combinations

You may be thinking about only one group.

1 group of 9 equals 9

→ 1 x 9 = 9

You may also be thinking about many groups of 1.

6 groups of 1 equal 6

→ 6 x 1 = 6

Learning the ×2 combinations

Multiplying by 2 is the same as doubling a number.

→ 8 + 8 = 16

→ 2 x 8 = 16

Learning the ×10 and ×5 combinations

You can learn these combinations by skip counting by 10s and 5s.

10, 20, 30, 40, 50, 60 → 6 x 10 = 60

5, 10, 15, 20, 25, 30 → 6 x 5 = 30

Another way to find a ×5 combination is to remember that it is half of a ×10 combination.

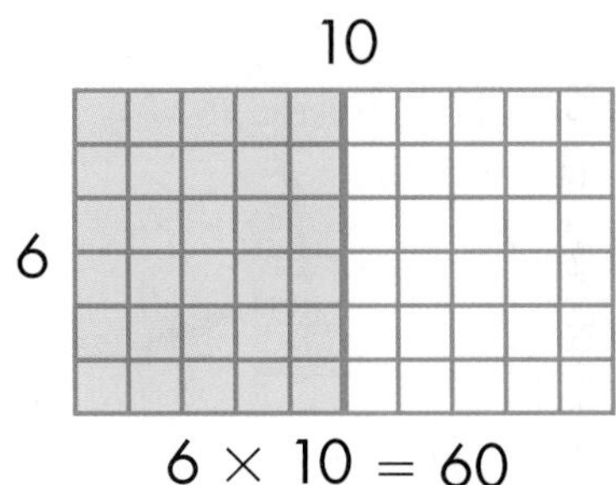

$6 \times 10 = 60$

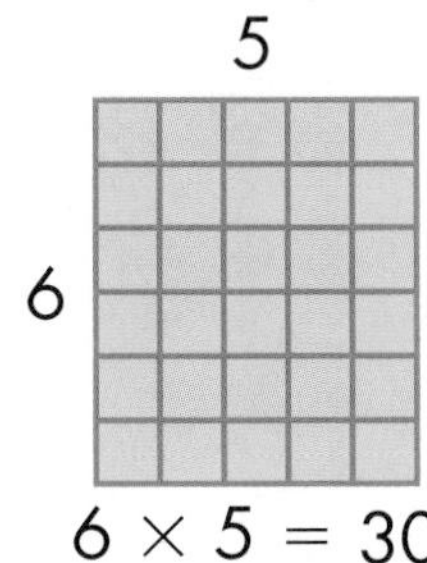

$6 \times 5 = 30$

6 x 5 (or 30) is half of 6 x 10 (or 60).

Multiplication Combinations (page 4 of 6)

Here are some more categories to help you learn the multiplication combinations.

Learning the ×11 Combinations

Many students learn these combinations by noticing the double-digit pattern they create.

11	11	11	11	11
x 3	x 4	x 5	x 6	x 7
33	44	55	66	77

Learning the ×12 Combinations

Many students multiply by 12 by breaking the 12 into 10 and 2.

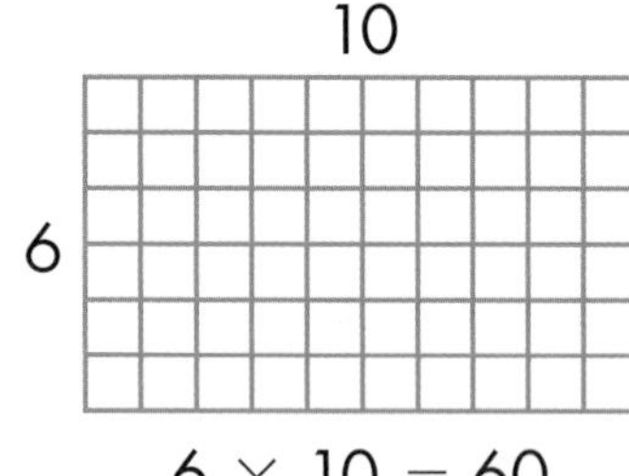

$6 \times 10 = 60$

2

6

$6 \times 2 = 12$

6 x 12 = (6 x 10) + (6 x 2)
6 x 12 = 60 + 12
6 x 12 = 72

Learning the Square Numbers

Many students remember the square number combinations from experiences building the squares with tiles or drawing them on grid paper.

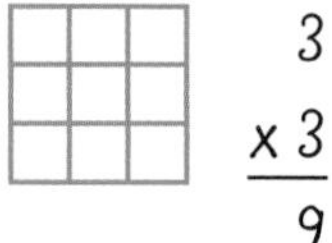

3 x 3 = 9

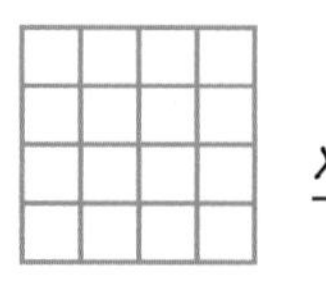

4 x 4 = 16

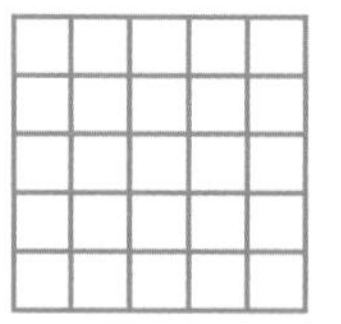

5 x 5 = 25

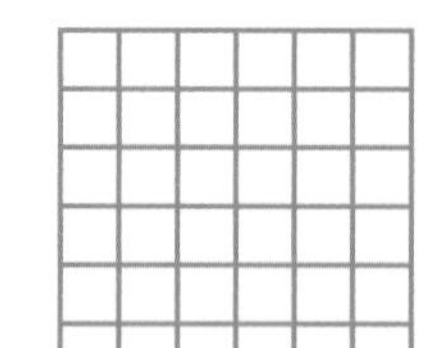

6 x 6 = 36

7 x 7 = 49

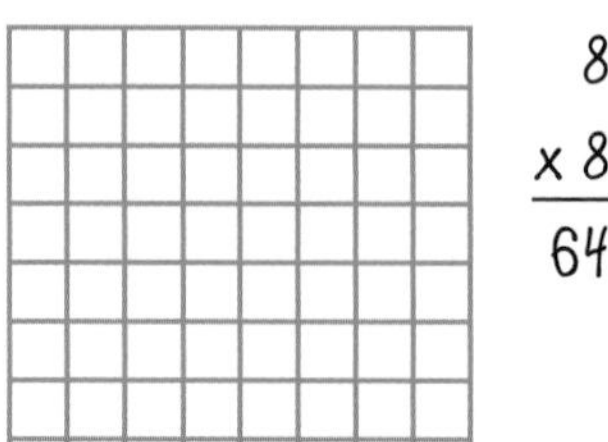

8 x 8 = 64

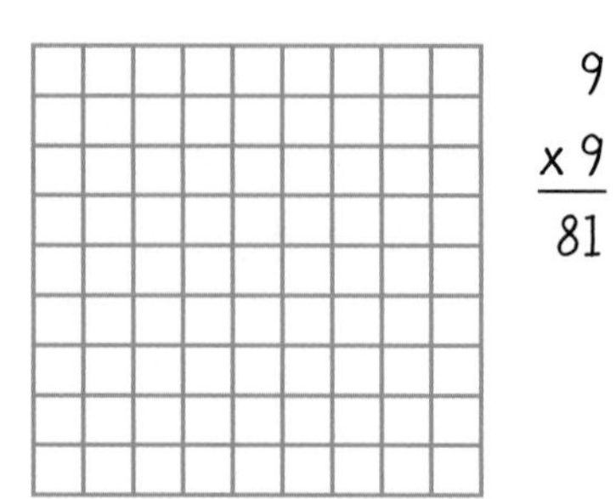

9 x 9 = 81

Multiplication Combinations (page 5 of 6)

After you have used all these categories to practice the multiplication combinations, you have only a few more to learn.

1 x 1	1 x 2	1 x 3	1 x 4	1 x 5	1 x 6	1 x 7	1 x 8	1 x 9	1 x 10	1 x 11	1 x 12
2 x 1	2 x 2	2 x 3	2 x 4	2 x 5	2 x 6	2 x 7	2 x 8	2 x 9	2 x 10	2 x 11	2 x 12
3 x 1	3 x 2	3 x 3	3 x 4	3 x 5	3 x 6	3 x 7	3 x 8	3 x 9	3 x 10	3 x 11	3 x 12
4 x 1	4 x 2	4 x 3 3 x 4	4 x 4	4 x 5	4 x 6	4 x 7	4 x 8	4 x 9	4 x 10	4 x 11	4 x 12
5 x 1	5 x 2	5 x 3	5 x 4	5 x 5	5 x 6	5 x 7	5 x 8	5 x 9	5 x 10	5 x 11	5 x 12
6 x 1	6 x 2	6 x 3 3 x 6	6 x 4 4 x 6	6 x 5	6 x 6	6 x 7	6 x 8	6 x 9	6 x 10	6 x 11	6 x 12
7 x 1	7 x 2	7 x 3 3 x 7	7 x 4 4 x 7	7 x 5	7 x 6 6 x 7	7 x 7	7 x 8	7 x 9	7 x 10	7 x 11	7 x 12
8 x 1	8 x 2	8 x 3 3 x 8	8 x 4 4 x 8	8 x 5	8 x 6 6 x 8	8 x 7 7 x 8	8 x 8	8 x 9	8 x 10	8 x 11	8 x 12
9 x 1	9 x 2	9 x 3 3 x 9	9 x 4 4 x 9	9 x 5	9 x 6 6 x 9	9 x 7 7 x 9	9 x 8 8 x 9	9 x 9	9 x 10	9 x 11	9 x 12
10 x 1	10 x 2	10 x 3	10 x 4	10 x 5	10 x 6	10 x 7	10 x 8	10 x 9	10 x 10	10 x 11	10 x 12
11 x 1	11 x 2	11 x 3	11 x 4	11 x 5	11 x 6	11 x 7	11 x 8	11 x 9	11 x 10	11 x 11	11 x 12
12 x 1	12 x 2	12 x 3	12 x 4	12 x 5	12 x 6	12 x 7	12 x 8	12 x 9	12 x 10	12 x 11	12 x 12

As you practice all of the multiplication combinations, there will be some that you "just know" and others that you are "working on" learning.

One way to practice a combination that is hard for you is to make a Multiplication Clue Card. Think of a combination you already know that you can start with to help you learn the harder one.

You will make your own Multiplication Cards for combinations that are hard for you.

On the next page are examples of Multiplication Cards made by students to help them learn 7×8 and 8×7.

7×8
8×7

Start with ____________

Multiplication Combinations (page 6 of 6)

Like many fourth graders, these students think that 7×8 is a hard multiplication combination to learn. Each of these students has a different strategy to solve 7×8. They use a multiplication combination that they know to help them solve 7×8.

Neomi: *I would do 7×7 and then add 7.*

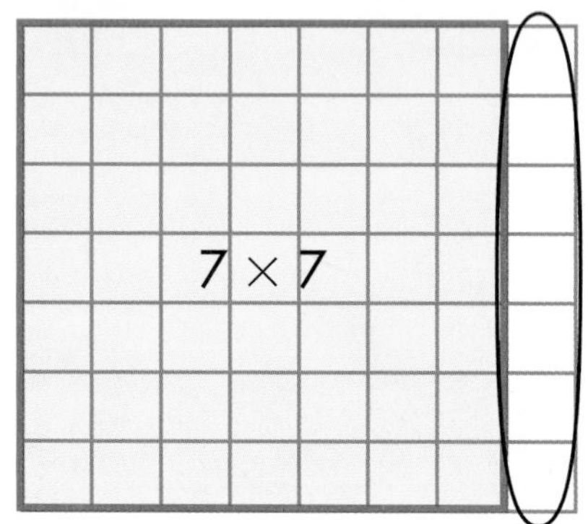

$$\begin{array}{r} 49 \\ +\ 7 \\ \hline 56 \end{array}$$

7×8
8×7
Start With 7 x 7
Neomi

Alejandro: *I would double a 7 by 4 array to make 7×8.*

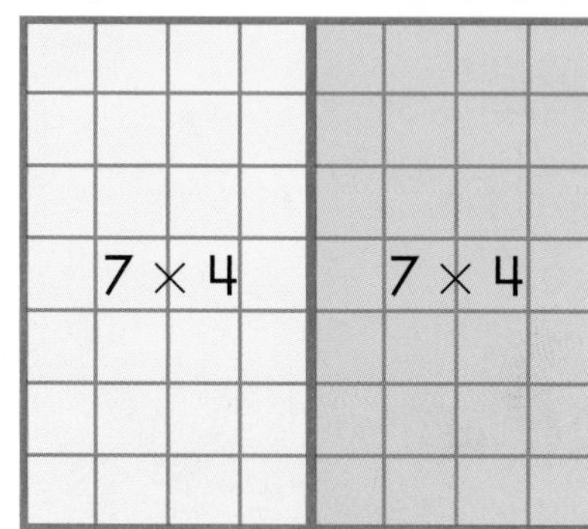

$$\begin{array}{r} 7 \\ \times\ 4 \\ \hline 28 \end{array}$$

$20 + 20 + 8 + 8 = 56$

$40 + 16 = 56$

7×8
8×7
Start With 7 x 4
Alejandro

Ramona: *I think of it as seven 8s. I would start at 5×8 and keep skip counting by 8s.*

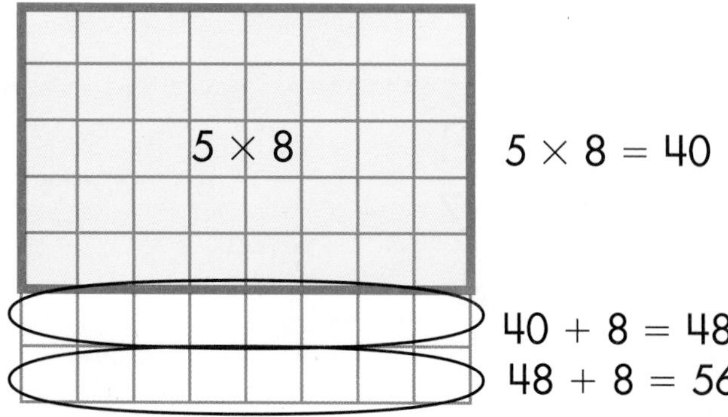

$5 \times 8 = 40$

$40 + 8 = 48$

$48 + 8 = 56$

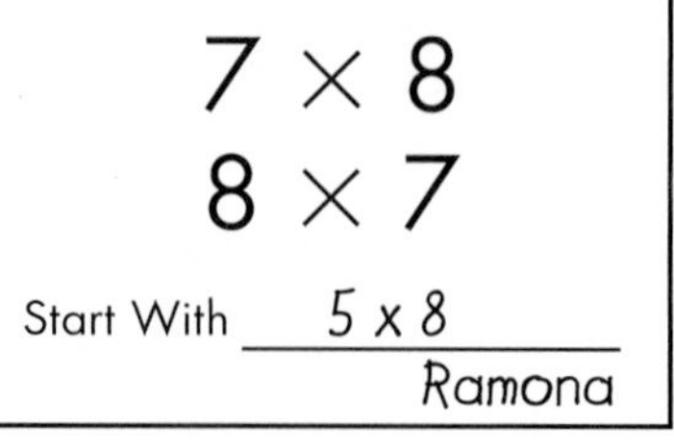

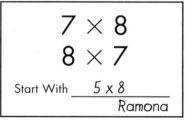

Multiplication Combinations and Related Division Problems

Think of the multiplication combinations that you know when you solve related division problems. You can review the multiplication combinations on pages 29–34.

$24 \div 6 =$ ____ Think $\underline{4} \times 6 = 24$ $24 \div 6 = \underline{4}$

$56 \div 7 =$ ____ Think $\underline{8} \times 7 = 56$ $56 \div 7 = \underline{8}$

$63 \div 9 =$ ____ Think $\underline{7} \times 9 = 63$ $63 \div 9 = \underline{7}$

$72 \div 12 =$ ____ Think $\underline{6} \times 12 = 72$ $72 \div 12 = \underline{6}$

What multiplication combination could help you solve this problem?
$45 \div 5 =$ ____

Multiple Towers

Math Words
- **multiple**

When you skip count by a certain number, you are finding multiples of that number.

Tonya's class made a multiple tower for the number 16. They recorded the multiples of 16 on a paper strip, starting at the bottom.

They circled every 10th multiple of 16 and used them as landmark multiples to solve the following problems.

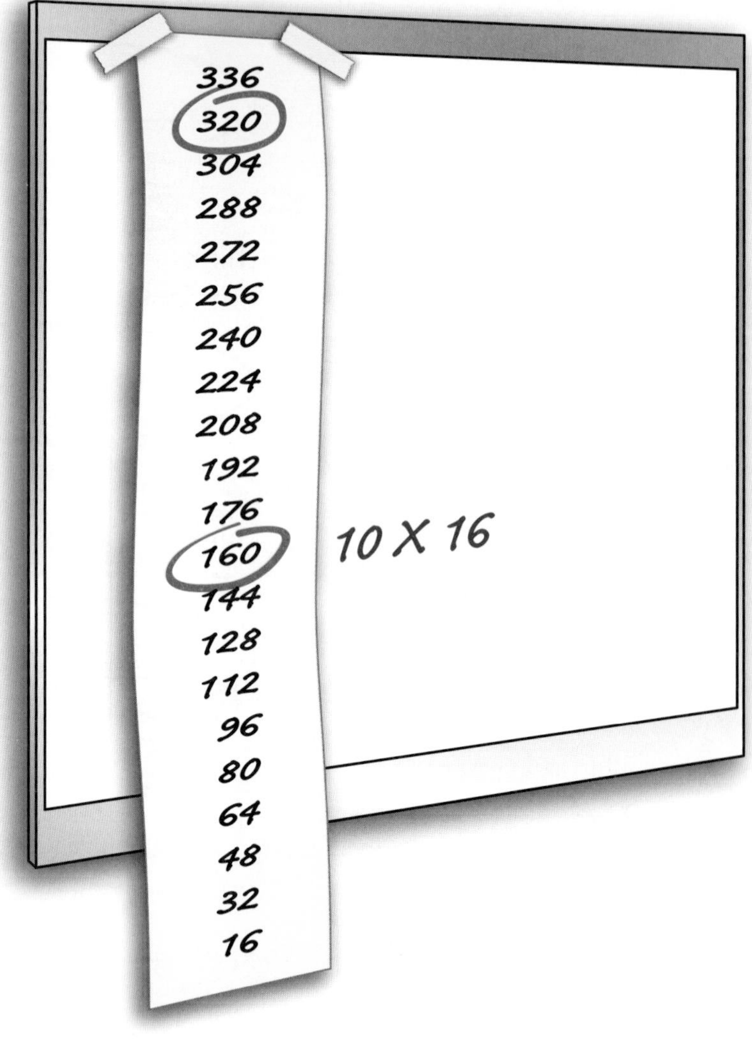

21 x 16 = 336

Tonya's solution

We know 20 × 16 = 320.
336 is next on the tower after 320, so it is one more 16.

30 x 16 = 480

Venetta's solution

30 x 16 would be the next landmark multiple on our tower. Since 3 × 16 = 48, then 30 × 16 = 48 × 10.

208 ÷ 16 = 13

Nadeem's solution

Ten 16s land on 160.
Three more 16s will go to 208.

How would you use this multiple tower to solve this problem?
11 × 16 = ______

Multiplying Groups of 10

(page 1 of 2)

Each of these models help show the relationship between these two multiplication equations.

$$3 \times 4 = 12$$

$$3 \times 40 = 120$$

Cubes

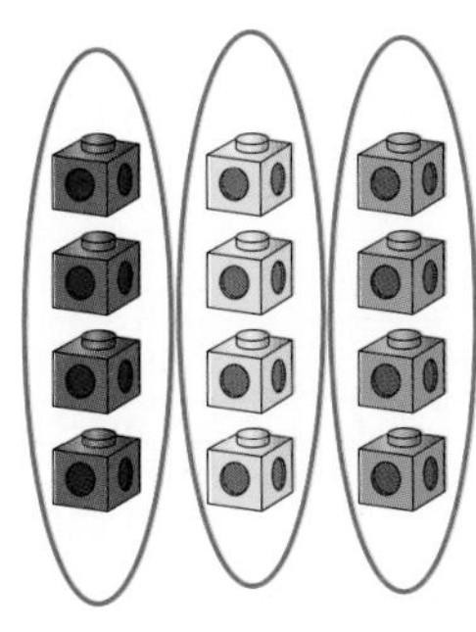

3 groups of 4 cubes

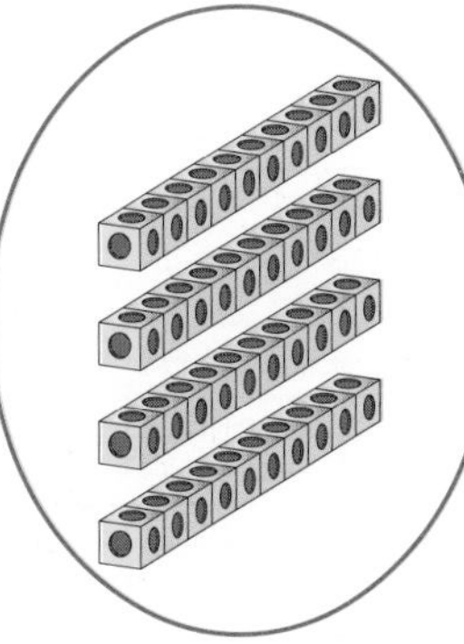

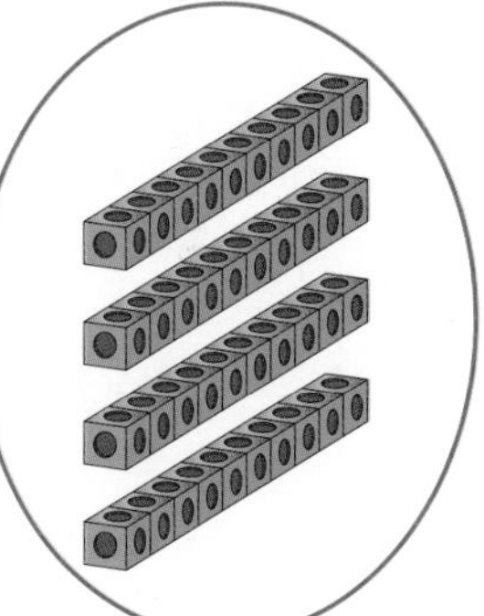

3 groups of 40 cubes

Arrays

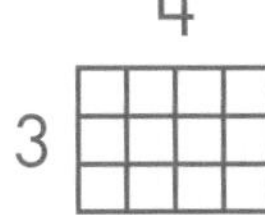

a 3 by 4 array

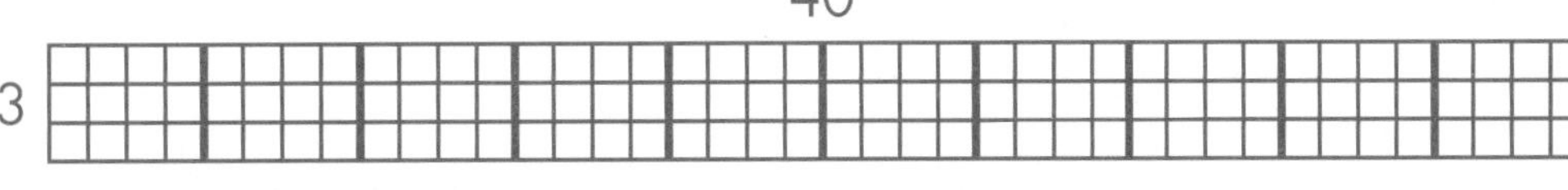

a 3 by 40 array

Skip Counting Patterns

This pattern of multiples increases by 4.

Multiples of 4: 4 8 (12) 16 20 24 28 32 36 40 . . .

This pattern of multiples increases by 4 tens.

Multiples of 40: 40 80 (120) 160 200 240 280 320 360 400 . . .

Multiplying Groups of 10

(page 2 of 2)

Consider the relationship among these three equations.

$3 \times 4 = 12$

$3 \times 40 = 120$

$30 \times 40 = 1{,}200$

$3 \times 4 = 12$	$3 \times 4 = 12$
$3 \times 40 = 120$	$(3 \times 4) \times 10 = 12 \times 10$
$30 \times 40 = 1{,}200$	$(3 \times 4) \times (10 \times 10) = 12 \times 100$

Solve these related problems.

5 × 7 = ______ 5 × 70 ______ 50 × 70 = ______

Multiplication Cluster Problems

Multiplication cluster problems are sets of multiplication problems that help you use what you know about easier problems to solve harder problems.

1. Solve the problems in each cluster.
2. Use one or more of the problems in the cluster to solve the final problem, along with other problems if you need them.

Solve these cluster problems.	How did you solve the final problem?
$2 \times 3 =$ 6 $5 \times 3 =$ 15 $50 \times 3 =$ 150	*I multiplied 50 by 3 and then the 2 by 3, and then I added.*
Now solve this problem. $52 \times 3 =$ **156**	*$50 \times 3 = 150$* *$2 \times 3 = 6$* ***156***

Solve these cluster problems.	How did you solve the final problem?
$4 \times 8 =$ 32 $20 \times 8 =$ 160 $25 \times 4 =$ 100	*I know that $25 \times 4 = 100$.* *Then I know that $25 \times 8 = 200$ because it is double.*
Now solve this problem. $24 \times 8 =$ **192**	*I need to subtract 8 because it is really 24×8.* *$200 - 8 =$* ***192***

Strategies for Solving Multiplication Problems

(page 1 of 4)

Breaking Numbers Apart

In Grade 4, you are learning how to solve multiplication problems with a 2-digit factor. In the examples on this page and page 41, students broke a multiplication problem with large numbers into smaller parts that made it easier to solve.

Steve and Kimberly solved the problem 28×4 by breaking the factor 28 into parts. Notice that the two students had two different ways to break apart 28.

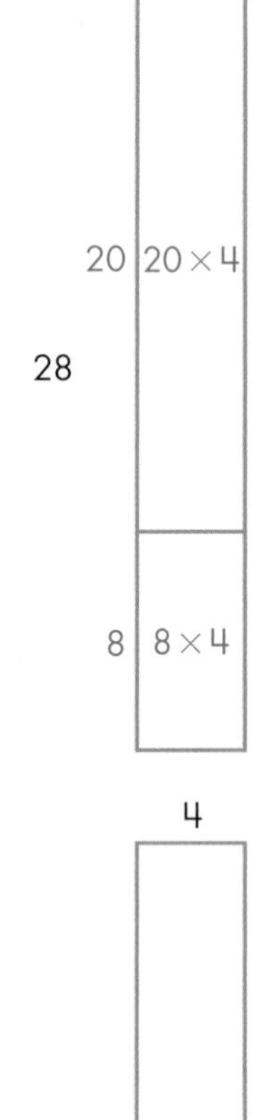

Steve's solution

$28 = 20 + 8$	*I broke 28 into 20 and 8.*
$20 \times 4 = 80$	*I used the 20 and multiplied 20 × 4.* *I know that 20 × 2 = 40 and 40 + 40 = 80.*
$8 \times 4 = 32$	*Next I needed to multiply 8 × 4.* *I know that multiplication combination.*
$80 + 32 =$ **112**	*For the last step I added 80 and 32.*

Kimberly's solution

$28 = 25 + 3$	*I broke 28 into 25 and 3.*
$25 \times 4 = 100$	*I used the 25 and multiplied 25 × 4.* *I know that 25 × 4 = 100 because 4 quarters equal $1.00.*
$3 \times 4 = 12$	*Next I needed to multiply 3 × 4.* *I know that multiplication combination.*
$100 + 12 =$ **112**	*For the last step, I added 100 and 12.*

Strategies for Solving Multiplication Problems

(page 2 of 4)

Richard solved the problem 38×26 by breaking apart both factors.

There are 38 rows in the auditorium with 26 chairs in each row. How many people can sit in the auditorium?

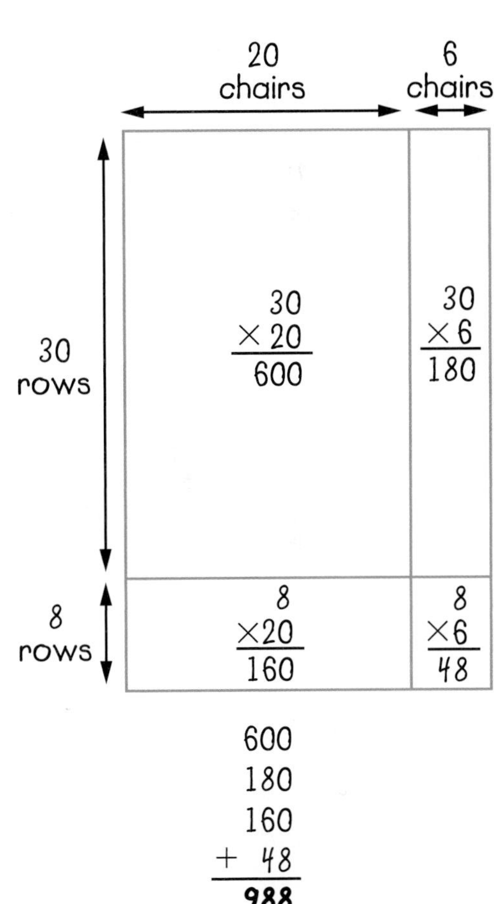

Richard's solution

How many people are in the first 30 rows?

$30 \times 20 = 600$ That's the first 30 rows, with 20 people in each row.

$30 \times 6 = 180$ That's 6 more people in each of those 30 rows, so now I've filled up 30 rows.

How many people are in the last 8 rows?

$8 \times 20 = 160$ That's 20 people in those last 8 rows.

$8 \times 6 = 48$ Now I've filled up the last 8 rows with 6 more people in each row.

How many people can sit in the auditorium?

$600 + 180 + 160 + 48 = \mathbf{988}$

988 people can sit in the auditorium.

Strategies for Solving Multiplication Problems

(page 3 of 4)

Changing One Number to Make an Easier Problem

Another way to solve multiplication problems is by changing one number to make the problem easier to solve. Amelia solved the auditorium problem, 38×26, by changing the 38 to 40 to make an easier problem.

Amelia's solution

I'll pretend that there are 40 rows in the auditorium instead of 38.

How many people could sit in 40 rows?

$40 \times 26 = 1{,}040$	*I know that $10 \times 26 = 260$. I doubled that to get 520, and doubled that to get 1,040.*

26 chairs

40 rows

$40 \times 26 = 1{,}040$

So, if there were 40 rows, 1,040 people could sit in the auditorium. But there are really only 38 rows, so I have 2 extra rows of 26 chairs. I need to subtract those.

$2 \times 26 = 52$	*I need to subtract 52. I'll do that in two parts.*
$1{,}040 - 40 = 1{,}000$	*First I'll subtract 40.*
$1{,}000 - 12 = $ ***988***	*Then I'll subtract 12.*

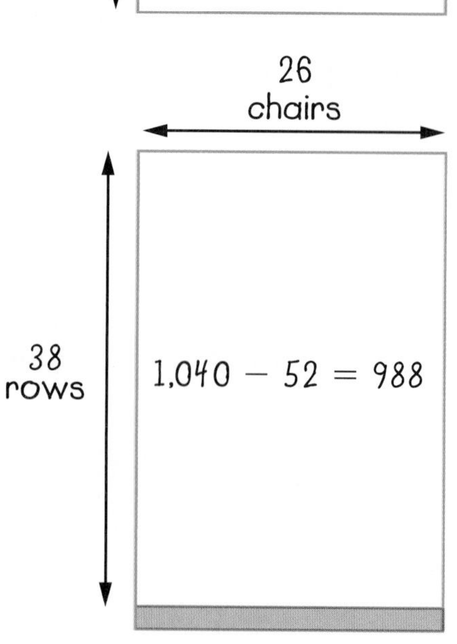

So, ***988*** *people can sit in the auditorium.*

Strategies for Solving Multiplication Problems

(page 4 of 4)

Creating an Equivalent Problem

One way to create an equivalent problem that is easier to solve is by "doubling and halving" the factors. Abdul solved the multiplication problem 6×35 by "doubling and halving" the factors to create the equivalent problem 70×3.

Abdul's solution

35 → 70		*I doubled 35 to get 70, and I took half*
x 6 → x 3		*of 6 to get 3.*
210		*My picture shows that $6 \times 35 = 3 \times 70$.*
		For me, 3×70 is an easier problem to solve.

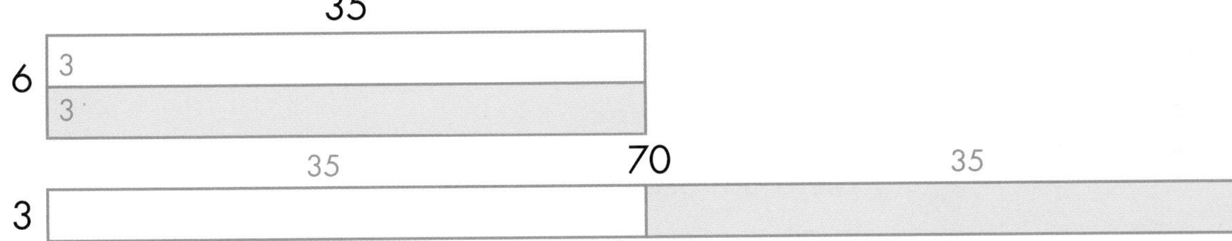

LaTanya solved the multiplication problem 4×36 by "tripling and thirding" the factors to create an equivalent problem.

LaTanya's solution

4 x 36 =	*I tripled 4 to get 12. $(4 \times 3 = 12)$*
↓ ↓	*I took a third of 36 to get 12. $(36 \div 3 = 12)$*
12 x 12 = **144**	*My picture shows that $4 \times 36 = 12 \times 12$.*
	For me, 12×12 is an easier problem to solve.

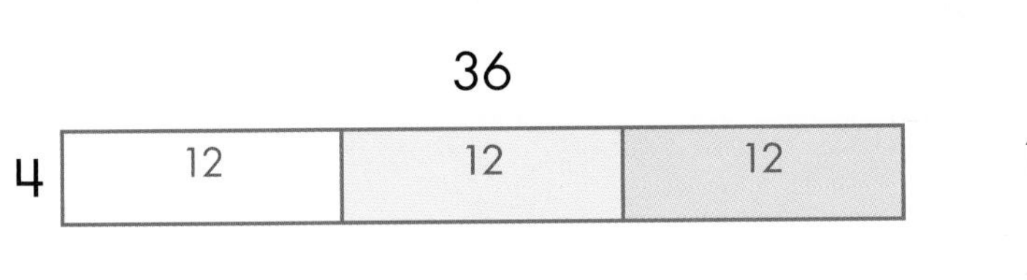

12

12

4

4

4

Division

Math Words
- **division**

Use division when you want to separate a total into equal-sized groups.

Ms. Santos owns a souvenir store. She has 36 water bottles to arrange on 4 shelves. How many water bottles will there be on each shelf if each shelf has the same number of bottles?

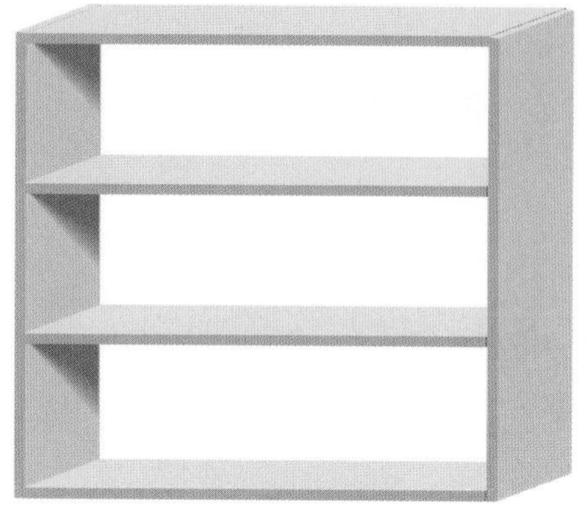

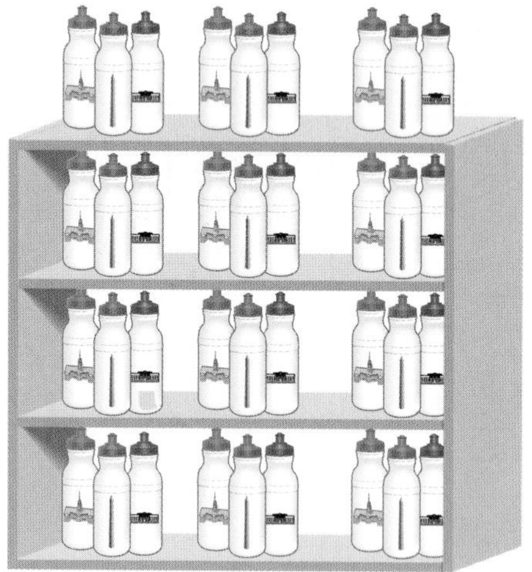

There are 36 water bottles in all.

There are 4 shelves.

Ms. Santos can display 9 water bottles on each shelf.

$$36 \div 4 = 9$$

total number of water bottles → 36; number of shelves → 4; number of water bottles on each shelf → 9

Division and Multiplication

Division and multiplication are related operations that both involve equal-sized groups.

× Use multiplication when you want to combine groups that are the same size.

Number of groups	Size of group	Number in all the groups	Equation
22 teams	18 players on each team	*unknown*	$22 \times 18 = \underline{\mathbf{396}}$

There are 22 youth soccer teams in our town, and there are 18 players on each team. How many players are on all of the teams?

Answer: There are **396** players in all.

÷ Use division when you want to separate a quantity into equal-sized groups.

Number of groups	Size of group	Number in all the groups	Equation
22 teams	*unknown*	396 players	$396 \div 22 = \underline{\mathbf{18}}$

There are 22 soccer teams in our town and 396 players altogether on all the teams. Each team has the same number of players. How many players are on each team?

Answer: Each team has **18** players.

Number of groups	Size of group	Number in all the groups	Equation
unknown	18 players on each team	396 players	$396 \div 18 = \underline{\mathbf{22}}$

There are 396 soccer players in our town, and there are 18 players on each team. How many teams are there?

Answer: There are **22** teams.

Division Situations

Look at this division expression: $28 \div 7$

There are two different kinds of division story problems we can think about.

The first type is a sharing situation.

There are 28 marbles being shared equally among 7 friends. How many marbles does each person get?

Each friend gets 4 marbles.

The second type is a grouping situation.

There are 28 marbles. I want to put 7 marbles in each bag. How many bags can I fill?

I can fill 4 bags.

Different symbols can be used to represent 28 divided by 7.

$28 \div 7$ $\qquad$ $7\overline{)28}$ $\qquad$ $\frac{28}{7}$ $\qquad$ $7 \times \underline{\ ?\ } = 28$

Write a story about $18 \div 3$.

Remainders

Math Words
- **remainder**

In some division problems the numbers do not divide evenly.

Look at this problem: 45 ÷ 6

My teacher has 45 pencils that she wants to tie together in groups of 6.

This problem has a remainder.

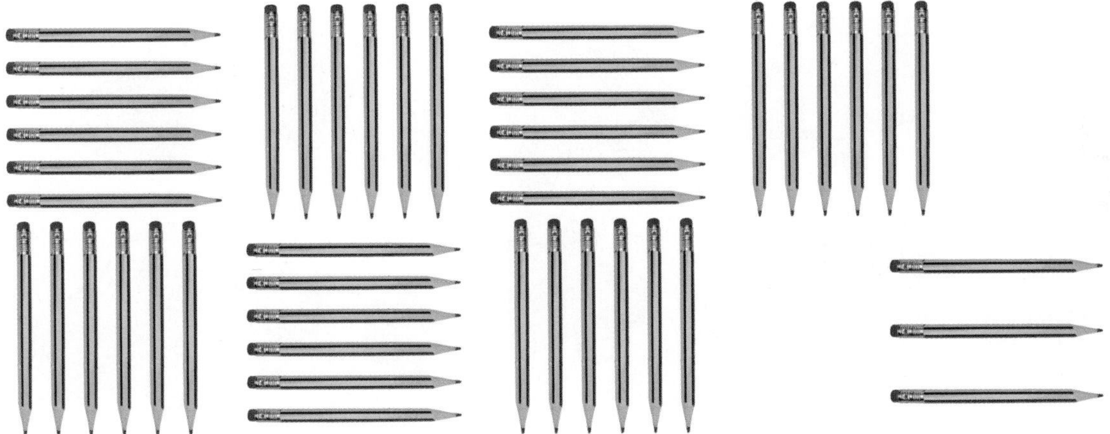

My teacher can make 7 groups of 6, and there are 3 pencils left over.

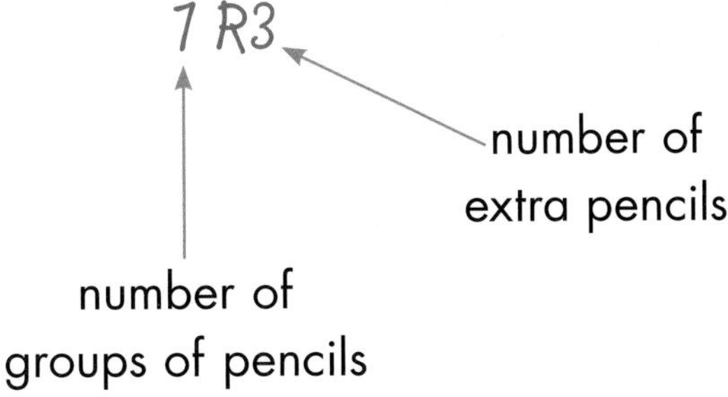

Steve has 22 apples. He wants to put them in bags with 4 to a bag. How many bags can he fill?

Remainders: What Do You Do with the Extras? (page 1 of 2)

These two pages show some different story problems for the division problem 30 ÷ 4. The answer to each problem is different, even though you divided the same numbers.

There are 30 people who are taking a car trip. Each car holds 4 people. How many cars do they need?

7 cars will hold 28 people, but the other 2 people still need a ride, so they need 1 more car.

Answer: They need **8** cars.

There are 30 pencils and 4 students. The teacher wants to give the same number to each student. How many does each student get?

It does not make sense to break up the leftover pencils to give to the students, so the teacher can keep the remaining 2 pencils.

Answer: Each student gets **7** pencils.

Remainders: What Do You Do with the Extras? (page 2 of 2)

Four friends earned $30 by washing people's cars. They want to share the money equally. How much does each person get?

Dollars can be split up into smaller amounts. Each person can get $7, and the $2 that are left can be divided evenly, so every person gets another 50¢.

Answer: Each person gets **$7.50.**

Four people are sharing 30 crackers evenly. How many crackers does each person get?

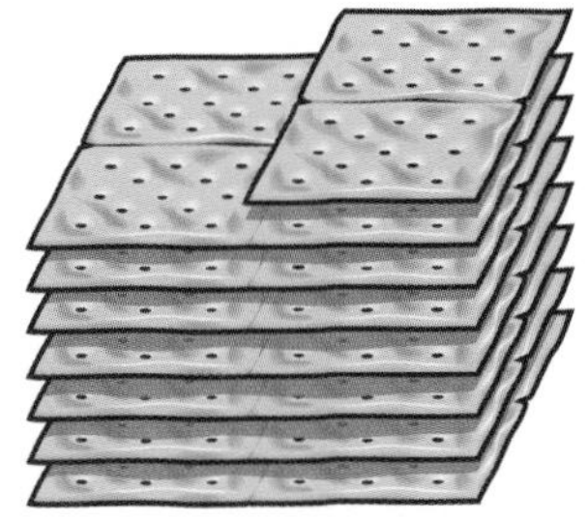
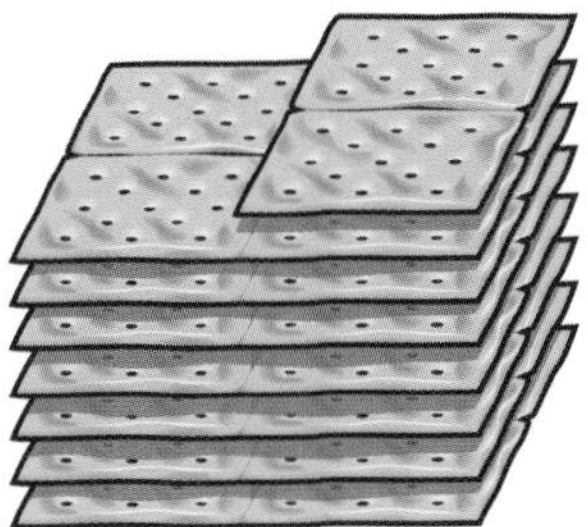
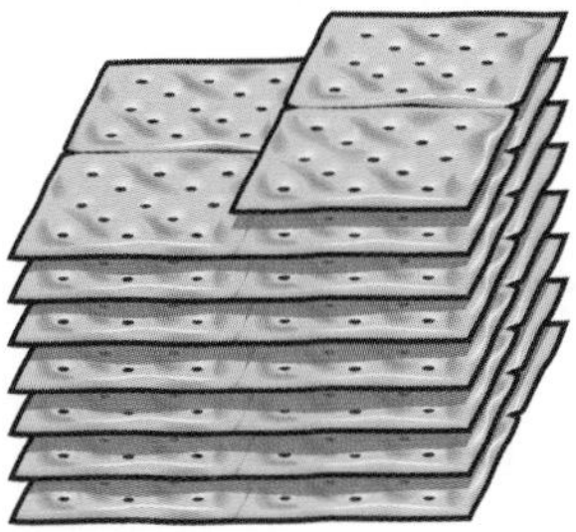
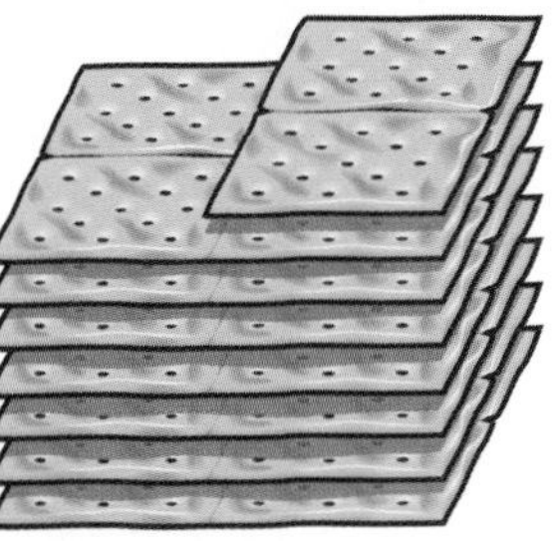

Each person gets 7 crackers. Then the last 2 crackers can be split in half. Each person gets another half cracker.

Answer: Each person gets $7\frac{1}{2}$ crackers.

What if the same problems involved these numbers? 186 ÷ 12
Write the new problems. Then tell what you would do with the extras.

Division Strategies (page 1 of 3)

In Grade 4, you are learning how to solve division problems efficiently.

$156 \div 13$

There are 156 students.
How many teams of 13 can they make?

Jake solved this problem by multiplying groups of 13 to reach 156.

Jake's solution

$10 \times 13 = 130$ *There are 130 students on 10 teams of 13.*

Team 1	Team 2	Team 3	Team 4	Team 5
13 students	13 students	13 students	13 students	13 students
Team 6	**Team 7**	**Team 8**	**Team 9**	**Team 10**
13 students	13 students	13 students	13 students	13 students

$156 - 130 = 26$ *There are 26 more students to put on teams.*

$2 \times 13 = 26$ *The 26 students make 2 more teams of 13.*

Team 11	Team 12
13 students	13 students

$10 + 2 = 12$ *10 teams plus 2 teams equal 12 teams.*

$12 \times 13 = 156$
$156 \div 13 = \mathbf{12}$ *The students can form **12** teams.*

Division Strategies (page 2 of 3)

Here is another solution to 156 ÷ 13. Ursula solved the problem by breaking up 156 and dividing the parts by 13.

Ursula's solution

156 = 130 + 26 *I broke up 156 into two parts that are easier to divide by 13.*

130 ÷ 13 = 10 *130 students make 10 teams of 13.*

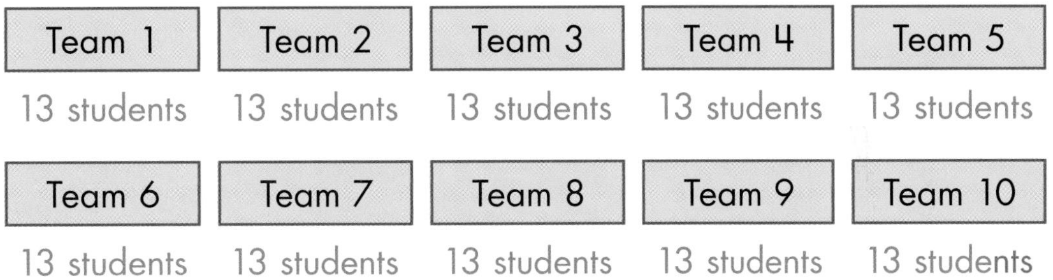

26 ÷ 13 = 2 *26 students make 2 teams of 13.*

Team 11	Team 12
13 students	13 students

10 + 2 = 12 *10 teams plus 2 teams equal 12 teams.*

*156 ÷ 13 = **12** The students can form **12** teams.*

Division Strategies (page 3 of 3)

Here are the ways that Emaan and Helena solved the following problem:

$14\overline{)240}$

Emaan solved the problem by breaking up 240 and dividing each part by 14.

Emaan's solution

240 = 140 + 70 + 30

140	÷	14	=	10
70	÷	14	=	5
28	÷	14	=	2
238	÷	14	=	17

Answer: **17 R2**

Helena solved the problem by multiplying groups of 14 to reach 240.

Helena's solution

10	x	14	=	140
2	x	14	=	28
2	x	14	=	28
2	x	14	=	28
1	x	14	=	14
17	x	14	=	238

Answer: **17 R2**

How would you solve this problem? $14\overline{)240}$

Fractions

Math Words
- **fraction**
- **numerator**
- **denominator**

Fractions are numbers.

Some fractions, like $\frac{1}{2}$ and $\frac{3}{4}$, are less than 1.

Some fractions, like $\frac{2}{2}$ and $\frac{4}{4}$, are equal to 1.

Some fractions, like $\frac{6}{4}$ and $\frac{3}{2}$, are greater than 1.

Fraction Notation

The denominator is the total number of equal shares. → $\frac{3}{4}$ ← The numerator is the number of equal shares out of the total.

three fourths

One third of Austria's flag is white.

The whole flag has three equal parts, or stripes. → $\frac{1}{3}$ ← One stripe is white.

1 out of 3 equal parts is white.

Four twelfths of these marbles are blue.

There are 12 marbles in the whole group. → $\frac{4}{12}$ ← Four of the marbles are blue.

4 out of 12 equal parts are blue.

What fraction of the flag is red?
What fraction of the marbles are green?

Fractions of an Area

Enrique, Helena, Amelia, and Luke have one sandwich to share equally. How much of the sandwich will each of them get?

Enrique cut the sandwich into 4 pieces. All of the pieces are the same size.

Each person gets $\frac{1}{4}$ of the sandwich.

Here are some other ways to cut one sandwich into fourths.

What other ways could you cut one sandwich into fourths?

Fractions of a Group of Objects

Three people shared 18 apples equally. Each person gets $\frac{1}{3}$ of the apples.

$\frac{1}{3}$ → 1 group for each person / 3 equal groups

- 1 → 1 group for each person
- 3 → 3 equal groups

$\frac{1}{3}$ of 18 is **6.**

There are 18 students in the dance club. Half of the students are girls.

- 1 → 1 group is girls
- 2 → 2 equal groups

$\frac{1}{2}$ of 18 is **9.**

Tonya bought a carton of 18 eggs. $\frac{5}{6}$ of them were cracked.

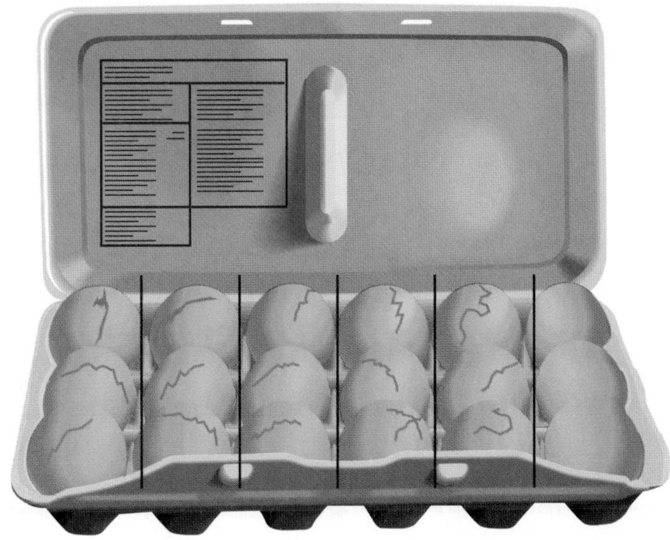

- 5 → 5 of the groups were cracked
- 6 → 6 equal groups

$\frac{5}{6}$ of 18 is **15.**

Naming Fractional Parts

(page 1 of 2)

In each of these examples, one whole square has been divided into equal parts.

How much is blue?
1 out of 2 equal parts

How much is white?
1 out of 2 equal parts

$\frac{1}{2}$

one half

$\frac{1}{2}$

one half

How much is blue?
1 out of 4 equal parts

How much is white?
3 out of 4 equal parts

$\frac{1}{4}$

one fourth
one quarter

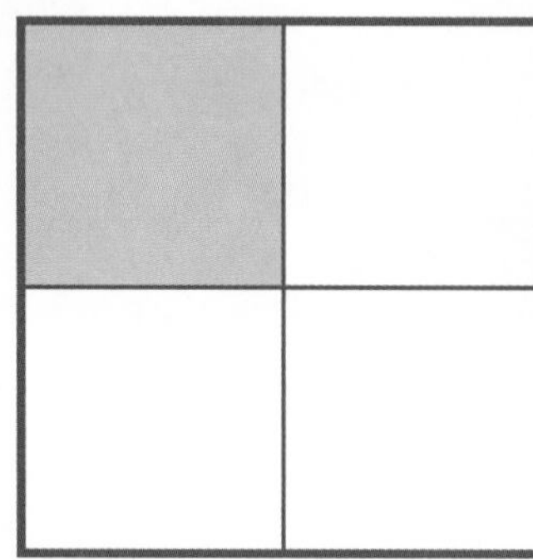

$\frac{3}{4}$

three fourths
three quarters

How much is blue?
1 out of 8 equal parts

How much is white?
7 out of 8 equal parts

$\frac{1}{8}$

one eighth

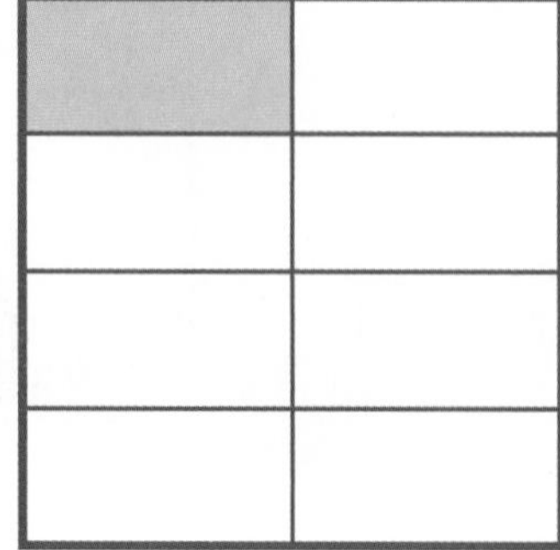

$\frac{7}{8}$

seven eighths

Naming Fractional Parts

(page 2 of 2)

How much is blue?
1 out of 3 equal parts

How much is white?
2 out of 3 equal parts

$\frac{1}{3}$

one third

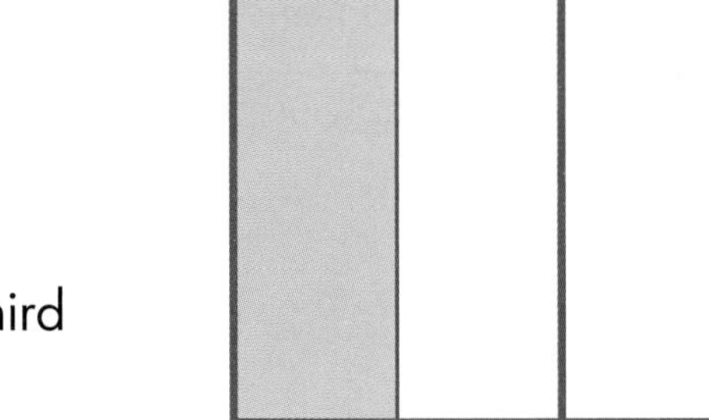

$\frac{2}{3}$

two thirds

How much is blue?
1 out of 6 equal parts

How much is white?
5 out of 6 equal parts

$\frac{1}{6}$

one sixth

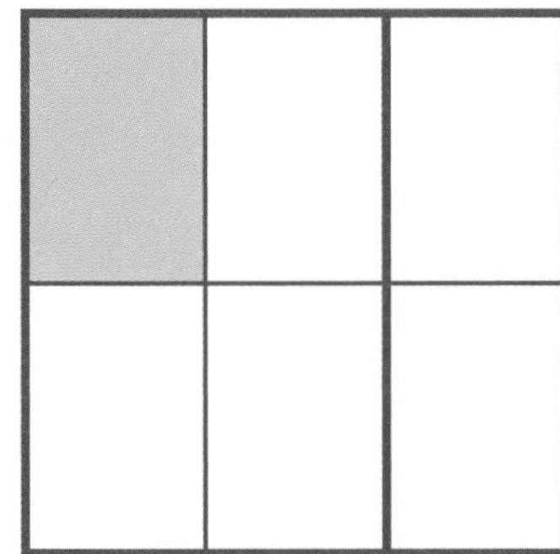

$\frac{5}{6}$

five sixths

Sabrina looked at all of these diagrams.

"It's interesting that 8 is the biggest number of parts, but that square has the smallest parts."

How much is shaded blue?
How much is shaded white?

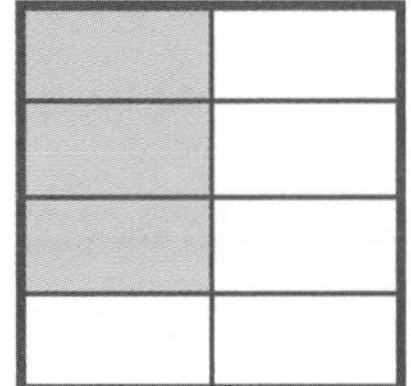

Using Fractions for Quantities Greater Than One

Math Words
- **mixed number**

To represent fractions greater than one, you need more than one whole.

In this diagram, each whole is divided into 6 equal parts. Six parts ($\frac{6}{6}$) are shaded on the first whole and one part ($\frac{1}{6}$) is shaded on the second whole.

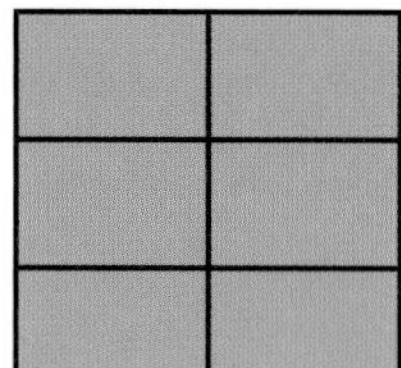
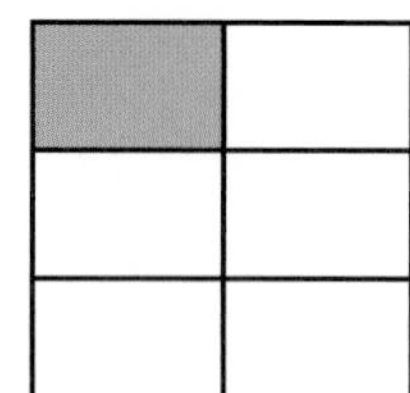

$\frac{7}{6}$ or $1\frac{1}{6}$

The total amount shaded is $\frac{7}{6}$, or $1\frac{1}{6}$.

In this diagram, two whole squares are shaded. That equals 2. It also equals $\frac{8}{4}$. (Imagine each of the two shaded wholes divided into fourths.)

The last square is divided into four equal parts, and three parts are shaded. That equals $\frac{3}{4}$.

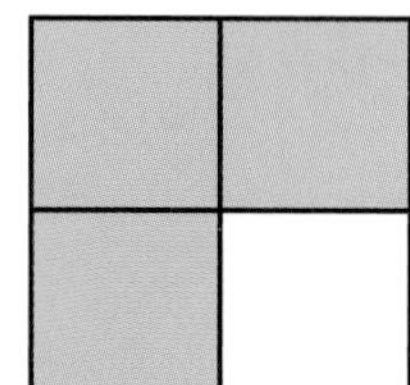

$2\frac{3}{4}$ or $\frac{11}{4}$

The total amount shaded is $\frac{11}{4}$ or $2\frac{3}{4}$.

A mixed number has a whole number part and a fractional part.

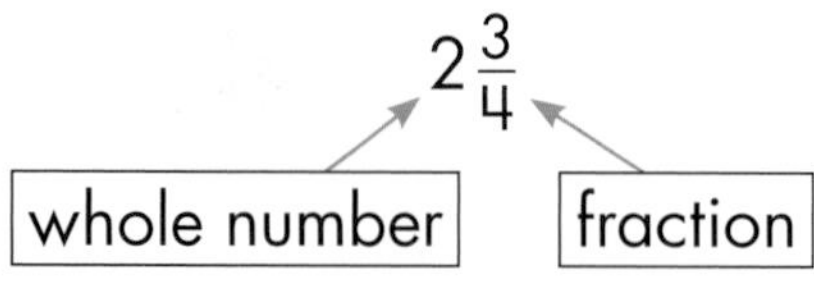

two and three fourths
two and three quarters

Show how you can represent these fractional parts using squares. $\frac{4}{3}$ $1\frac{3}{8}$

Equivalent Fractions

Math Words

- **equivalent fractions**

Different fractions that name the same amount are called equivalent fractions.

Benson used 4 × 6 rectangles to show some equivalent fractions.

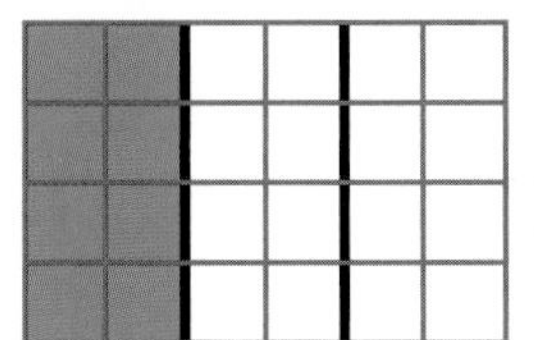

$\frac{1}{3} = \frac{2}{6}$

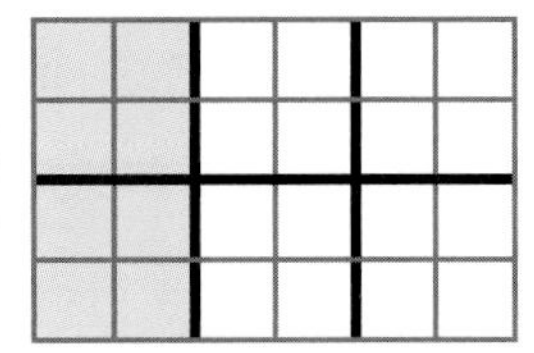

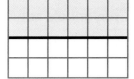

I just split the thirds in half to get sixths.

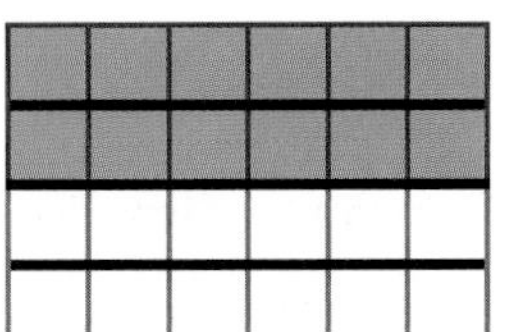

$\frac{2}{4} = \frac{1}{2}$

I just combined the fourths to get halves.

Helena showed some other equivalent fractions using whole squares.

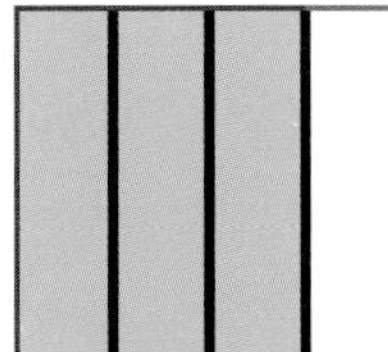

$\frac{3}{4} = \frac{6}{8}$

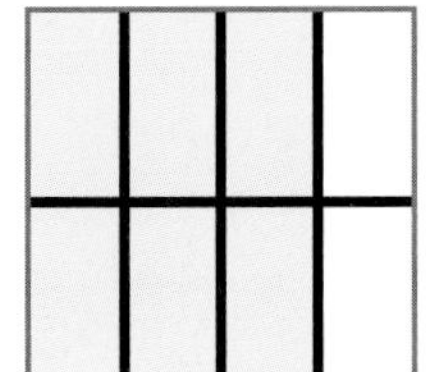

$1\frac{1}{2} = \frac{6}{4}$

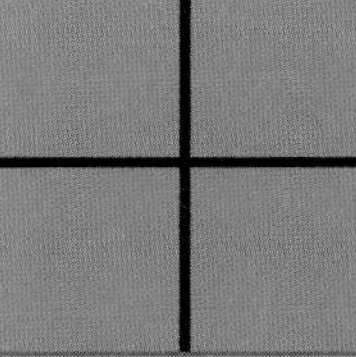

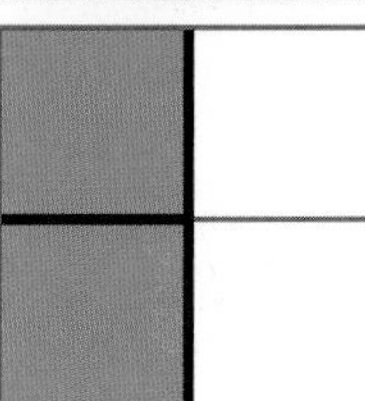

Jake showed that $\frac{1}{6} = \frac{4}{24}$ using a group of marbles.

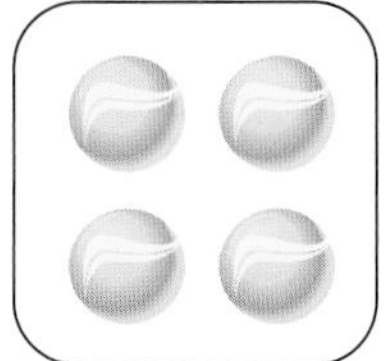
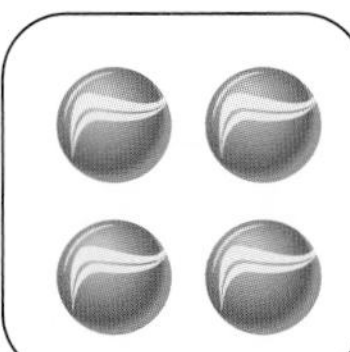
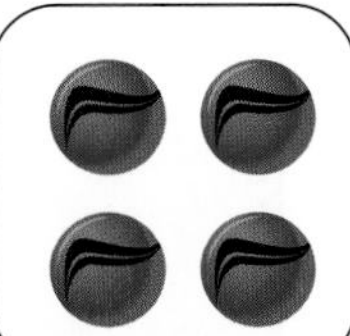
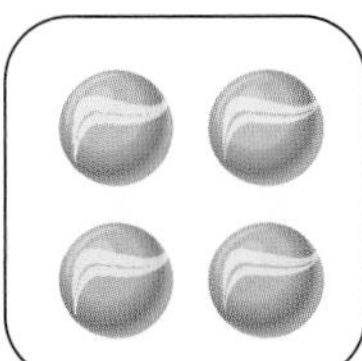
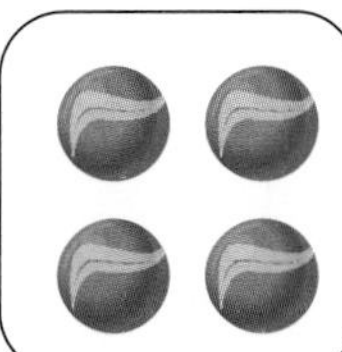
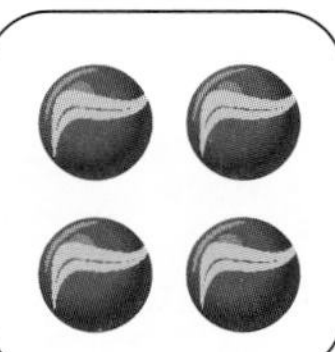

If 6 friends share 24 marbles equally, each person gets ***4*** *marbles.*
Each person's share is $\frac{1}{6}$ *or* $\frac{4}{24}$*.*

What two equivalent fractions name the portion of red cubes?

Comparing Fractions

(page 1 of 2)

Which is larger, $\frac{2}{5}$ or $\frac{5}{2}$?

Cheyenne drew pictures to solve the problem.

Cheyenne's solution

$\frac{2}{5}$ is less than 1 whole.

I drew $\frac{2}{5}$ by dividing the whole into 5 equal parts and then I shaded 2 parts.

$\frac{2}{5}$

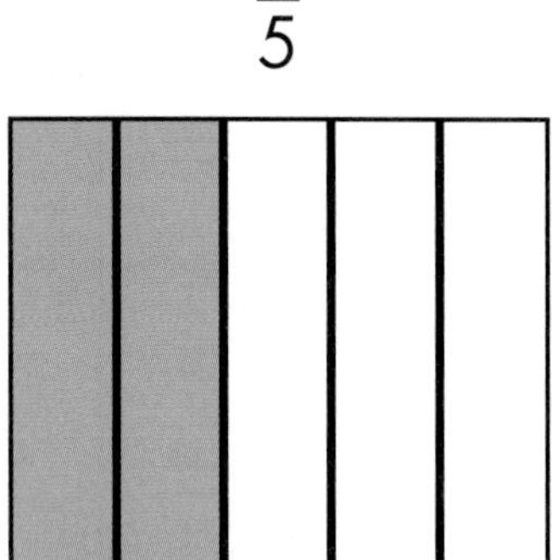

I needed 3 wholes to draw $\frac{5}{2}$. Each whole is divided in half and then I shaded 5 halves.

$\frac{5}{2}$

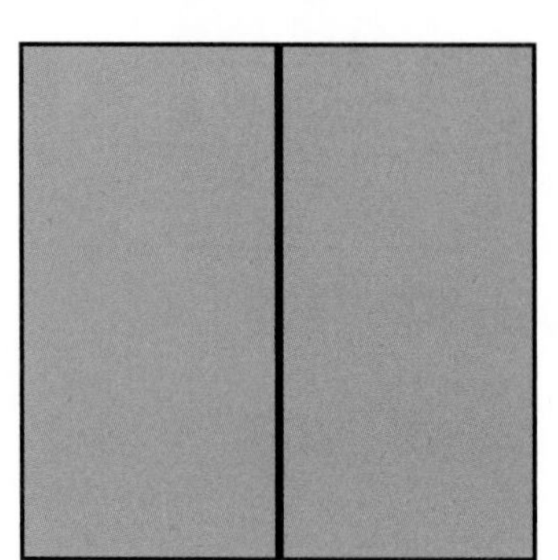

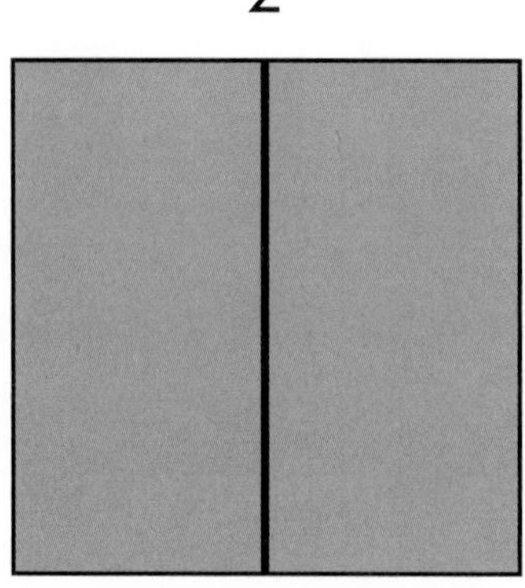

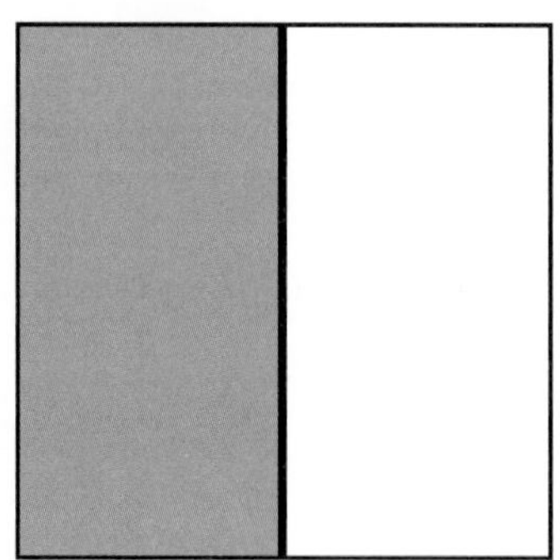

My pictures show that $\frac{5}{2}$ is larger than $\frac{2}{5}$.

$$\mathbf{\frac{5}{2} > \frac{2}{5}}$$

Comparing Fractions

(page 2 of 2)

Which is larger, $\frac{7}{8}$ or $\frac{5}{6}$?

Alejandro drew pictures to solve the problem.

Alejandro's solution

I shaded $\frac{7}{8}$ and $\frac{5}{6}$ on 4×6 grids.

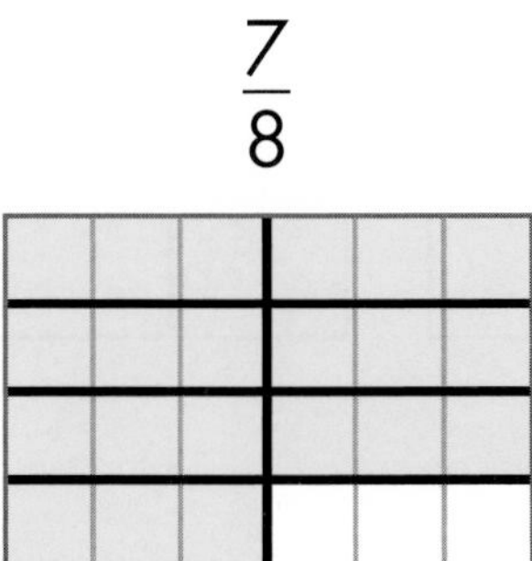
7/8

5/6

$\frac{1}{8}$ is missing from the whole.

$\frac{1}{6}$ is missing from the whole.

Because $\frac{7}{8}$ is missing a smaller piece, $\frac{7}{8}$ is larger than $\frac{5}{6}$. $\mathbf{\frac{7}{8} > \frac{5}{6}}$

Fractions can also be compared on a number line.

Which is larger, $\frac{4}{8}$ or $\frac{6}{4}$?

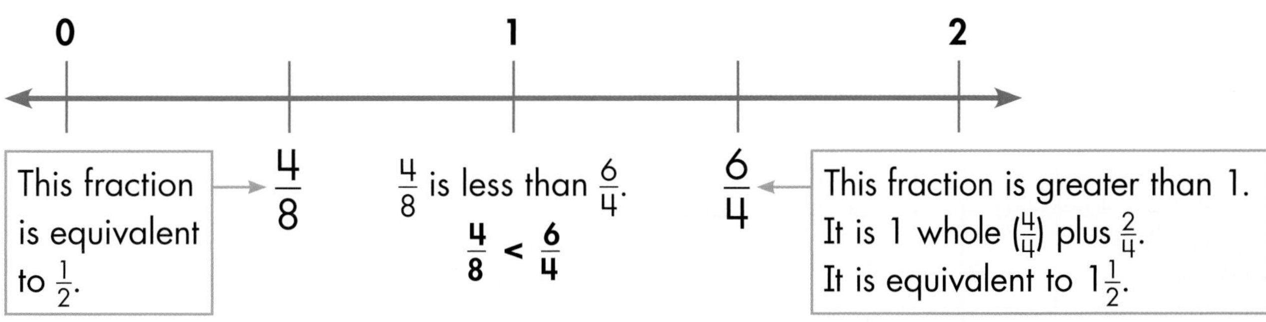
0
1
2
This fraction is equivalent to $\frac{1}{2}$.
$\frac{4}{8}$
$\frac{4}{8}$ is less than $\frac{6}{4}$.
$\frac{4}{8} < \frac{6}{4}$
$\frac{6}{4}$
This fraction is greater than 1. It is 1 whole ($\frac{4}{4}$) plus $\frac{2}{4}$. It is equivalent to $1\frac{1}{2}$.

Which is larger, $\frac{1}{2}$ or $\frac{5}{8}$?

Adding Fractions

These students used representations to solve problems about adding fractions.

Kimberly had 24 baseball cards. She gave $\frac{1}{8}$ of the cards to her sister and $\frac{3}{8}$ of the cards to a friend. What fraction of her cards did Kimberly give away?

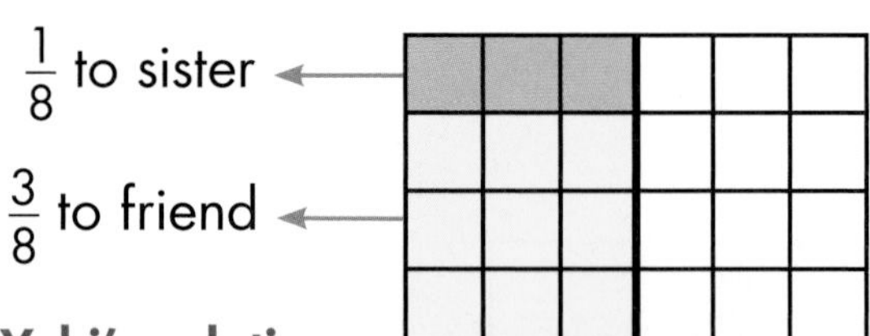

Yuki's solution

I used a 4 × 6 rectangle to solve the problem. The rectangle has 24 squares, just like Kimberly's 24 baseball cards. I shaded $\frac{1}{8}$ blue and $\frac{3}{8}$ yellow.

$$\frac{1}{8} + \frac{3}{8} = \frac{4}{8} \text{ or } \mathbf{\frac{1}{2}}$$

Kimberly gave away half of her cards.

Adam and Jill each ate part of the same sandwich. Adam ate $\frac{1}{2}$ of the sandwich. Jill ate $\frac{1}{4}$ of the sandwich. What is the total amount of the sandwich they ate?

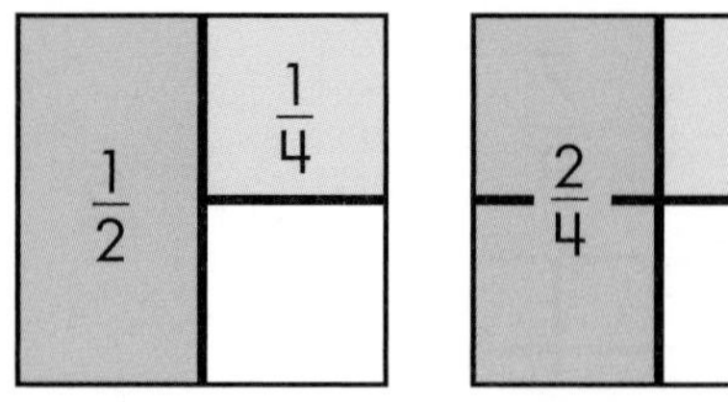

Anya's solution

I know that $\frac{1}{2}$ is equal to $\frac{2}{4}$, so I added $\frac{2}{4} + \frac{1}{4}$.

$$\frac{2}{4} + \frac{1}{4} = \mathbf{\frac{3}{4}}$$

Adam and Jill ate $\frac{3}{4}$ of the sandwich.

Fill in the blank to make the equation true.

$\frac{1}{3} + \frac{1}{6} +$ ______ $= 1$

Derek's solution

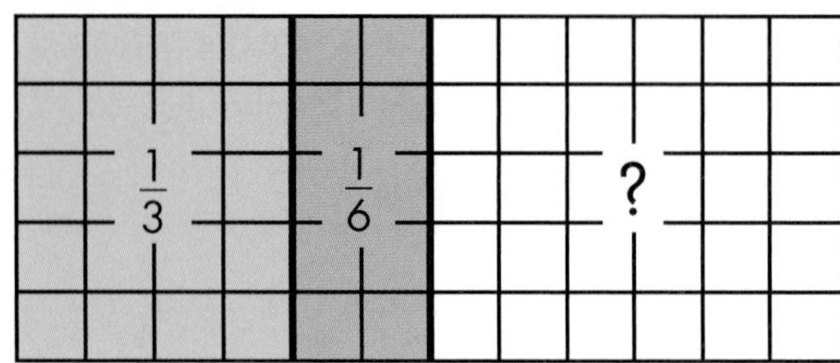

I used a 5 × 12 rectangle to solve the problem.

$\frac{1}{3}$ covers 20 out of 60 square units and $\frac{1}{6}$ covers 10 square units. That leaves 30 square units, which is $\frac{1}{2}$ of the rectangle. The missing fraction is $\frac{1}{2}$.

$$\frac{1}{3} + \frac{1}{6} + \mathbf{\frac{1}{2}} = 1$$

Halves of Different Wholes

Steve shaded $\frac{1}{2}$ of this 4×6 rectangle.

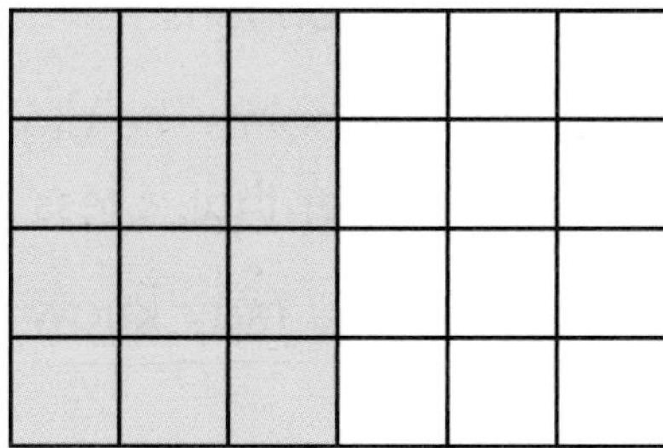

Steve's solution

I know that the shaded part is $\frac{1}{2}$ because the whole rectangle has 24 square units and the shaded part has 12 square units, and $2 \times 12 = 24$.

Ramona shaded $\frac{1}{2}$ of this 5×12 rectangle.

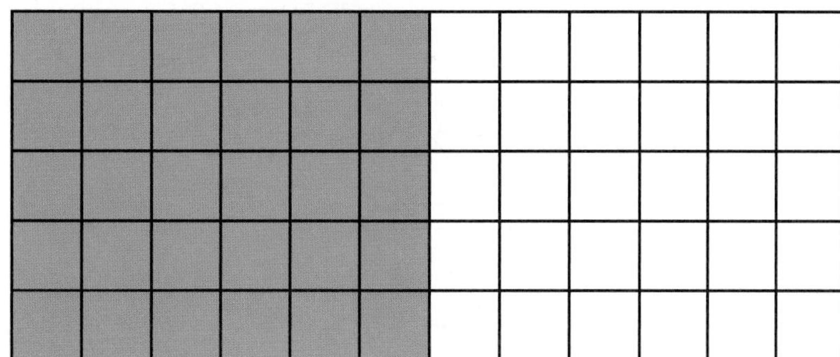

Ramona's solution

I know that the shaded part is $\frac{1}{2}$ because I drew a line in the middle of the rectangle. There are 30 shaded squares and 30 unshaded squares.

Half of the 4×6 rectangle is smaller than half of the 5×12 rectangle because the whole 4×6 rectangle is smaller than the whole 5×12 rectangle.

How many square units are in $\frac{1}{2}$ of this 10×10 square?

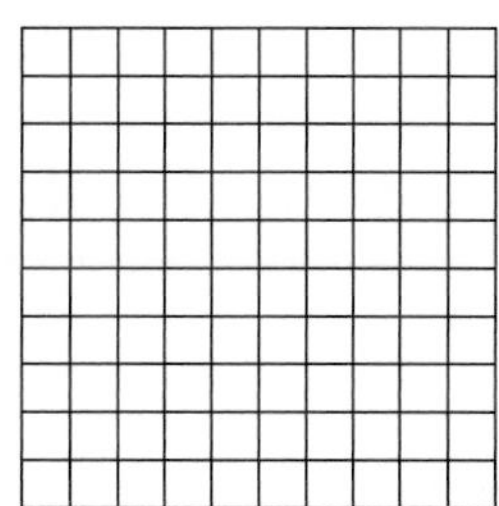

Decimals

Math Words
- **decimal**
- **decimal point**

The system we use to write numbers is called the decimal number system. *Decimal* means that the number is based on tens.

Some numbers, like 2.5 and 0.3, include a decimal point. The digits to the right of the decimal point are the part of the number that is less than 1.

Here are some examples of decimal numbers you may know that are less than one.

$0.5 = \frac{5}{10} = \frac{1}{2}$	$0.25 = \frac{25}{100} = \frac{1}{4}$

Numbers such as 0.5 and 0.25 are sometimes called decimal fractions.

Some decimal numbers have a whole number part and a part that is less than 1, just as mixed numbers do.

$1.5 = 1\frac{5}{10} = 1\frac{1}{2}$	$12.75 = 12\frac{75}{100} = 12\frac{3}{4}$

Here are some examples of the ways we use decimals everyday:

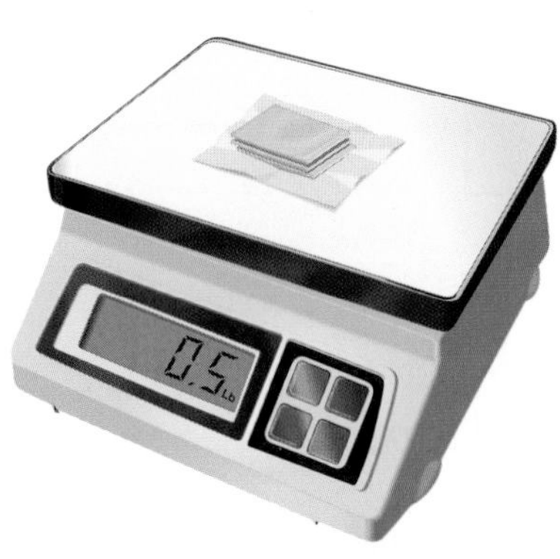

Derek bought 0.5 pound of cheese.

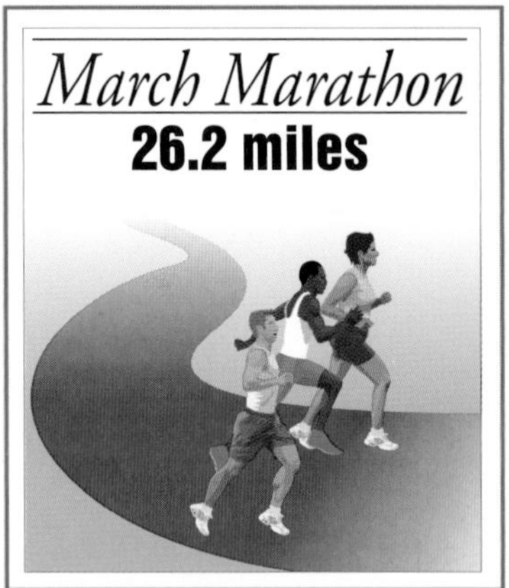

The race is a little more than 26 miles.

The T-shirt costs a little less than $10.

Write a decimal number that is. . . a little more than 5.
. . . almost 17.
. . . more than $\frac{1}{2}$ and less than 1.

Representing Decimals

Math Words

- **one tenth**
- **one hundredth**
- **one thousandth**

This square represents one whole.

In each of the following examples, the whole square has been divided into equal parts and the amount shaded is named.

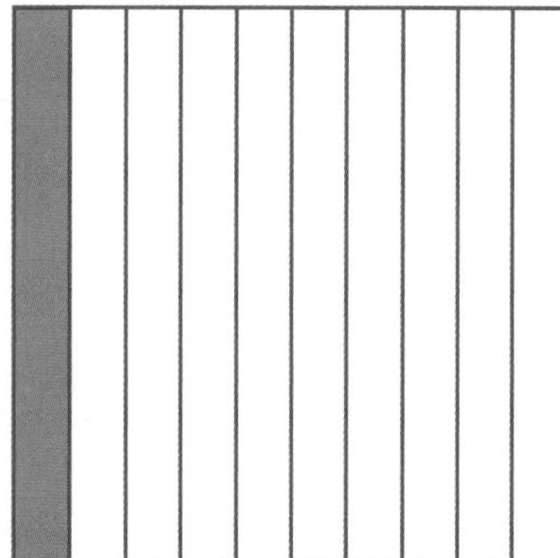

This square is divided into 10 parts.

One out of the ten parts is shaded.

Amount shaded: one tenth

fraction: $\frac{1}{10}$

decimal: 0.1

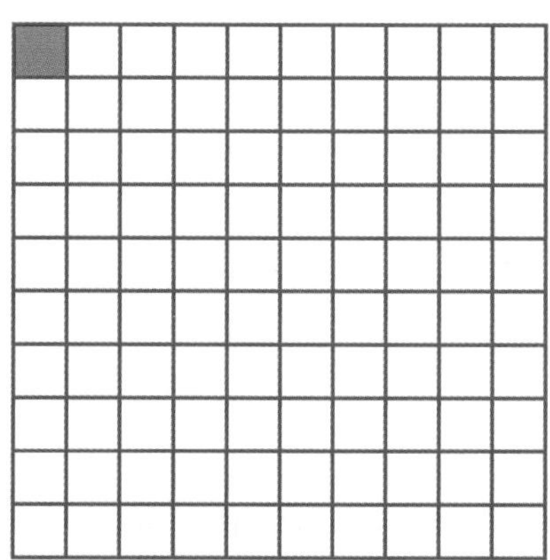

This square is divided into 100 parts.

One out of the 100 parts is shaded.

Amount shaded: one hundredth

fraction: $\frac{1}{100}$

decimal: 0.01

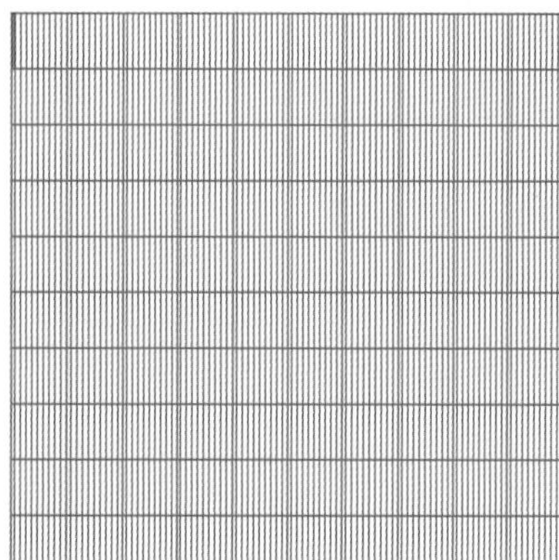

This square is divided into 1,000 parts.

One out of the 1,000 parts is shaded.

Amount shaded: one thousandth

fraction: $\frac{1}{1000}$

decimal: 0.001

Place Value of Decimals

(page 1 of 2)

Math Words
- **place value**
- **decimal point**

As with whole numbers, the value of a digit changes depending on its place in a decimal number.

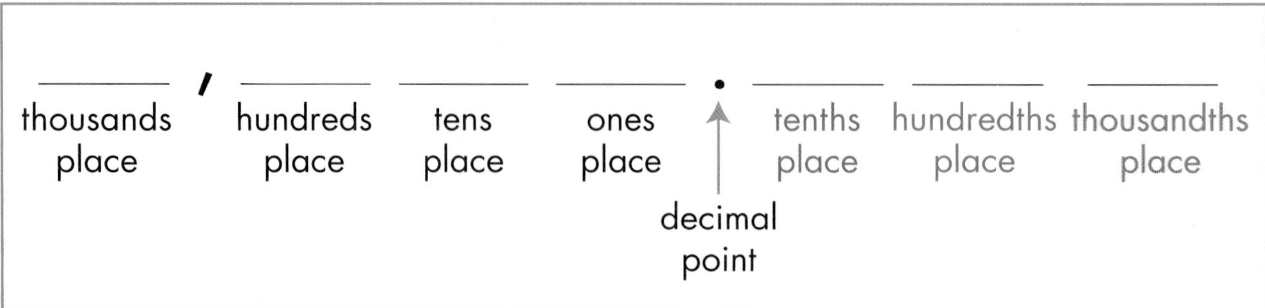

In these two examples, the digit 5 has different values.

0.<u>5</u>

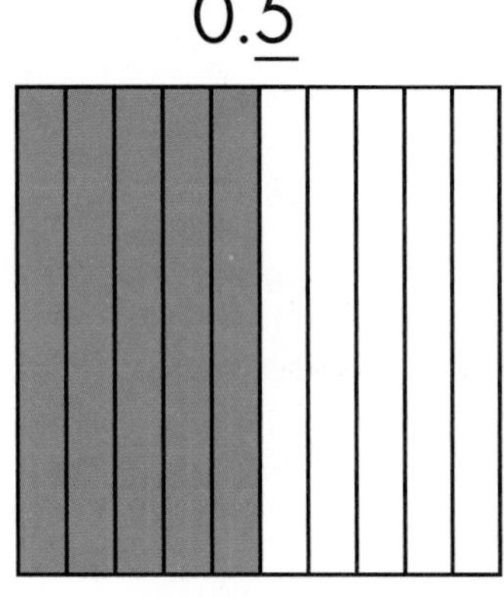

The digit 5 in the tenths place represents $\frac{5}{10}$.

0.4<u>5</u>

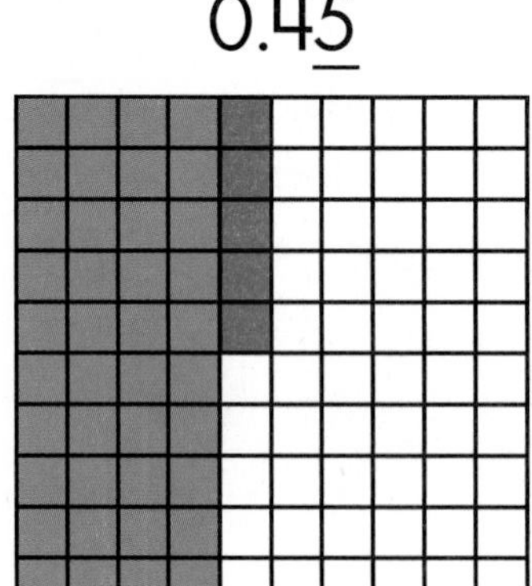

The digit 5 in the hundredths place represents $\frac{5}{100}$.

What are the values of the digits in this number? 0.39

Place Value of Decimals

(page 2 of 2)

Look at the values of the digits in this number:

2.75

two and seventy-five hundredths

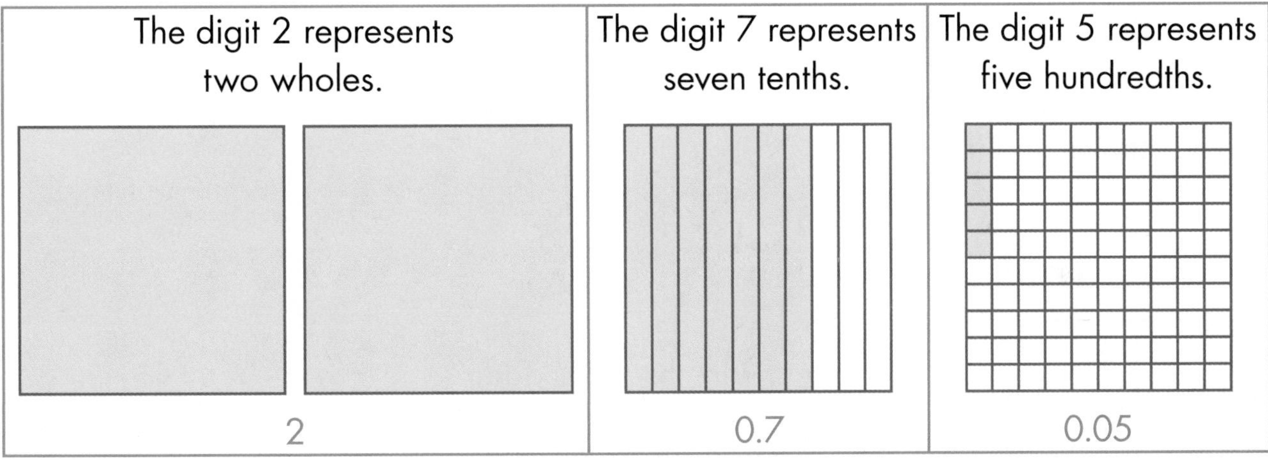

The digit 2 represents two wholes.	The digit 7 represents seven tenths.	The digit 5 represents five hundredths.
2	0.7	0.05

$2.75 = 2 + 0.7 + 0.05$

For decimals greater than one, read the whole number, say "and" for the decimal point, then read the decimal.

Here are some more examples:

10.5	200.05	17.45
ten and five tenths	two hundred and five hundredths	seventeen and forty-five hundredths

How would you say this number?

40.35

How would you write this number?

three hundred five and four tenths

Tenths and Hundredths

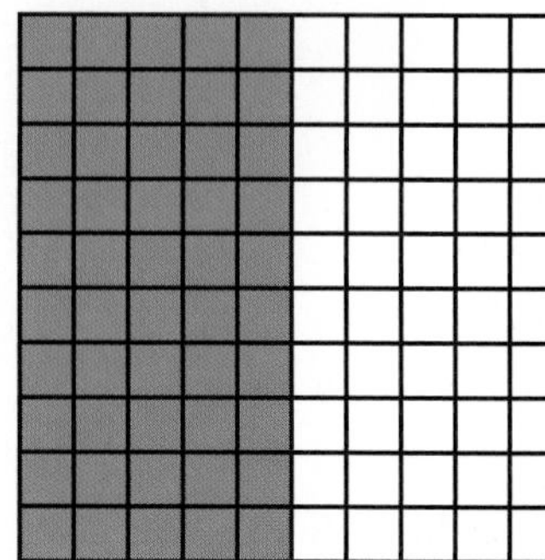

How many tenths are shaded?

0.5 5 out of 10 columns are shaded.

How many hundredths are shaded?

0.50 50 out of 100 squares are shaded.

These decimals are equal: $0.5 = 0.50$

There are many ways to represent the same part of a whole with decimals and fractions.

$$0.5 = 0.50 = \frac{1}{2} = \frac{5}{10} = \frac{50}{100}$$

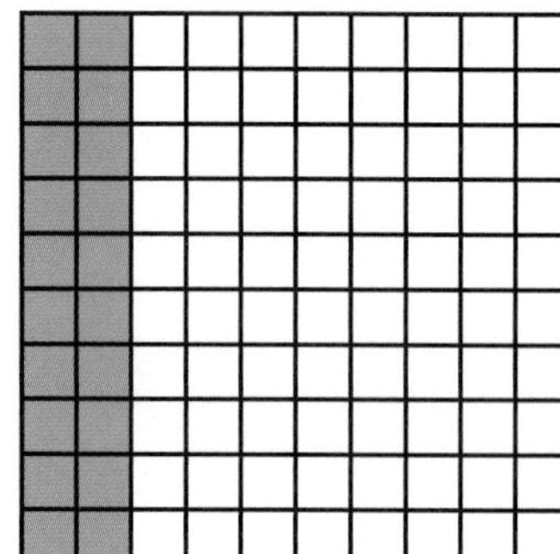

How many tenths are shaded?

0.2 2 out of 10 columns are shaded.

How many hundredths are shaded?

0.20 20 out of 100 squares are shaded.

$$0.2 = 0.20 = \frac{2}{10} = \frac{1}{5} = \frac{20}{100}$$

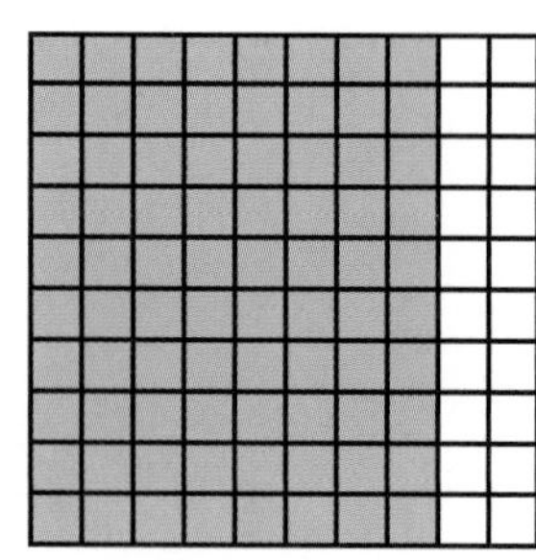

How many tenths are shaded?
How many hundredths are shaded?
What fractional part is shaded?

Comparing Decimals

Anna and Luke both walk to school from their homes.

Anna walks 0.35 miles.

Luke walks 0.6 miles.

Who walks farther?

LaTanya's solution

I used a number line from 0 to 1. First I marked $\frac{1}{2}$. Then I marked tenths. I know that $\frac{1}{2}$ mile is the same as 0.5. Luke walks 0.6 miles, which is a little more than $\frac{1}{2}$. Anna walks 0.35 miles, which is between 0.3 and 0.4 miles and is less than $\frac{1}{2}$. So, Luke walks farther than Anna.

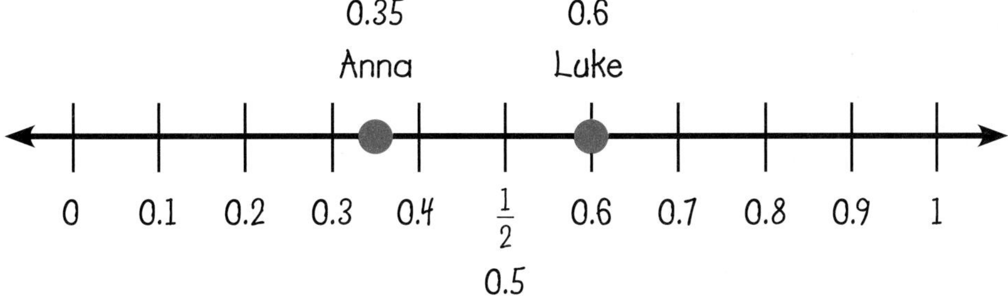

Kimberly's solution

0.35 is three and a half tenths.

0.6 is six tenths, so it is larger.

Damian's solution

I thought 0.35 was bigger because it has more numbers in it. But when I drew the picture I saw that 0.6 is the same as $\frac{60}{100}$, which is greater than $\frac{35}{100}$.

35 is greater than 6, but 0.35 is not greater than 0.6.

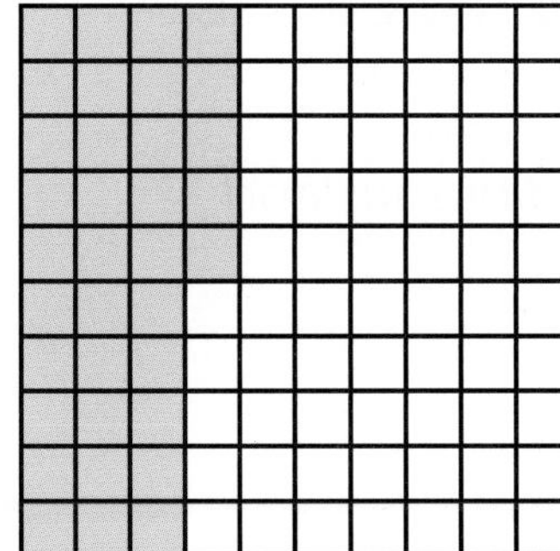

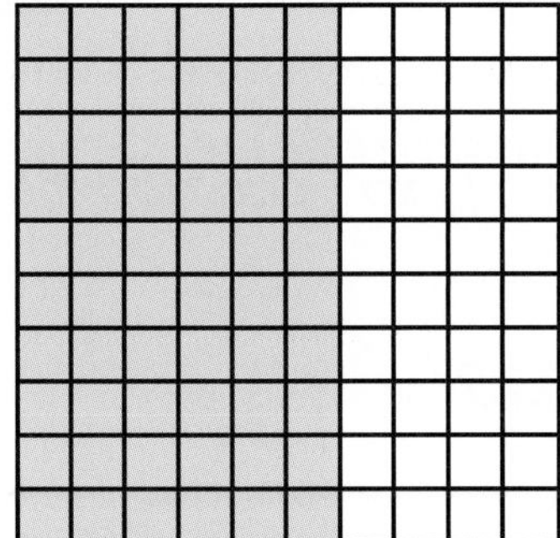

$0.35 < 0.6$

Adding Decimals (page 1 of 2)

$0.5 + 0.6 =$

Helena's solution

I added 0.5 and 0.6.

0.5 is $\frac{1}{2}$. 0.6 is $\frac{1}{2}$ and one more tenth.

So 5 tenths plus 6 tenths equal one whole and one tenth.
*$0.5 + 0.6 =$ **1.1***

I checked my work by shading the decimals on these 10×10 squares.

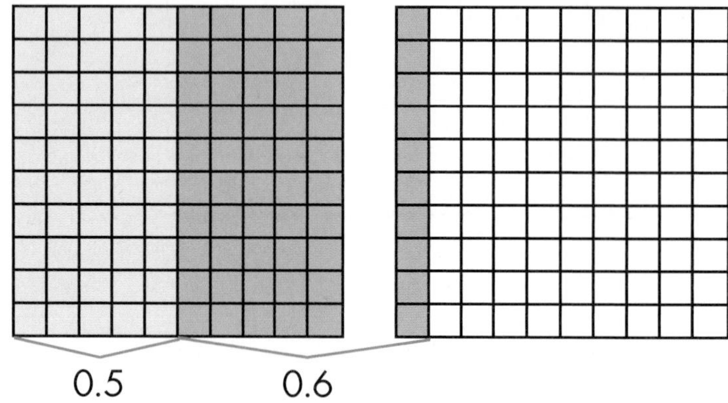

$0.5 + 0.25 =$

Bill's solution

I shaded both decimals on a 10×10 square, using different colors.

I shaded 0.5 in green. I shaded 0.25 in blue.

That is 2 more tenths and 5 hundredths.

*The total is 7 tenths and 5 hundredths or **0.75**.*

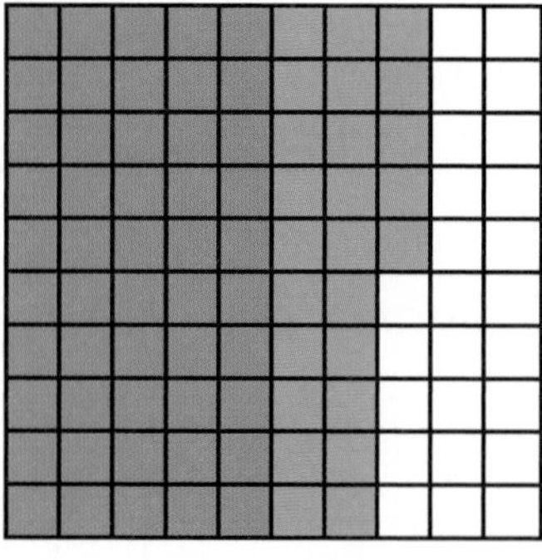

Marisol's solution

I know that $0.5 = \frac{1}{2}$ and $0.25 = \frac{1}{4}$, so I can add the fractions instead and get the same answer.

*$\frac{1}{2} + \frac{1}{4} = \frac{3}{4}$. $\frac{3}{4}$ is the same as **0.75**.*

Adding Decimals (page 2 of 2)

Nadeem and Amelia get exercise everyday by going for a walk together. They keep track of their walking in a log in which they record how far they walk each day. Here is the beginning of one of their walking logs.

Day	How Far Did We Walk?
Monday	2.5 miles
Tuesday	2 miles
Wednesday	1.2 miles

How far have they walked so far this week?

Nadeem's solution

I added the whole miles first:

2 (from 2.5), 2, and 1 (from 1.2). $2 + 2 + 1 = 5$

Next I added the tenths:

Five tenths plus two tenths equals seven tenths. $0.5 + 0.2 = 0.7$

Then I combined 5 miles and 0.7 miles.

$$\begin{array}{r} 5 \\ +\ 0.7 \\ \hline \mathbf{5.7} \end{array}$$ **miles**

Amelia's solution

I thought about fractions to solve the problem.

$2.5 = 2\frac{5}{10}$

$1.2 = 1\frac{2}{10}$

$2\frac{5}{10} + 1\frac{2}{10} = 3\frac{7}{10}$

$3 + 2 = 5$

$5 + \frac{7}{10} = \mathbf{5\frac{7}{10}}$

2.5 miles

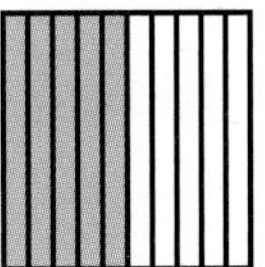

2 miles

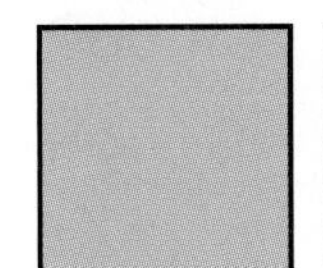

1.2 miles

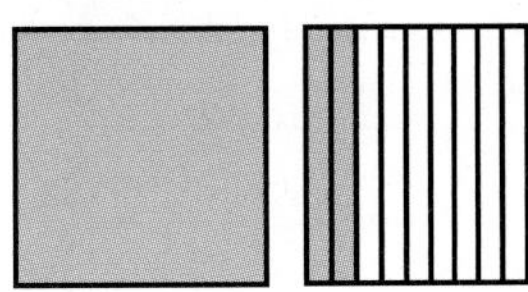

Graphs

Math Words
- **line graph**
- **horizontal axis (*x*-axis)**
- **vertical axis (*y*-axis)**

This line graph shows how the temperature changed in Norfolk over time from December 8 to December 14.

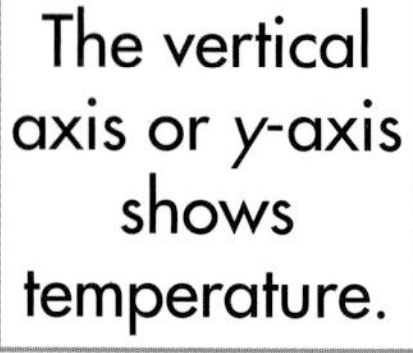

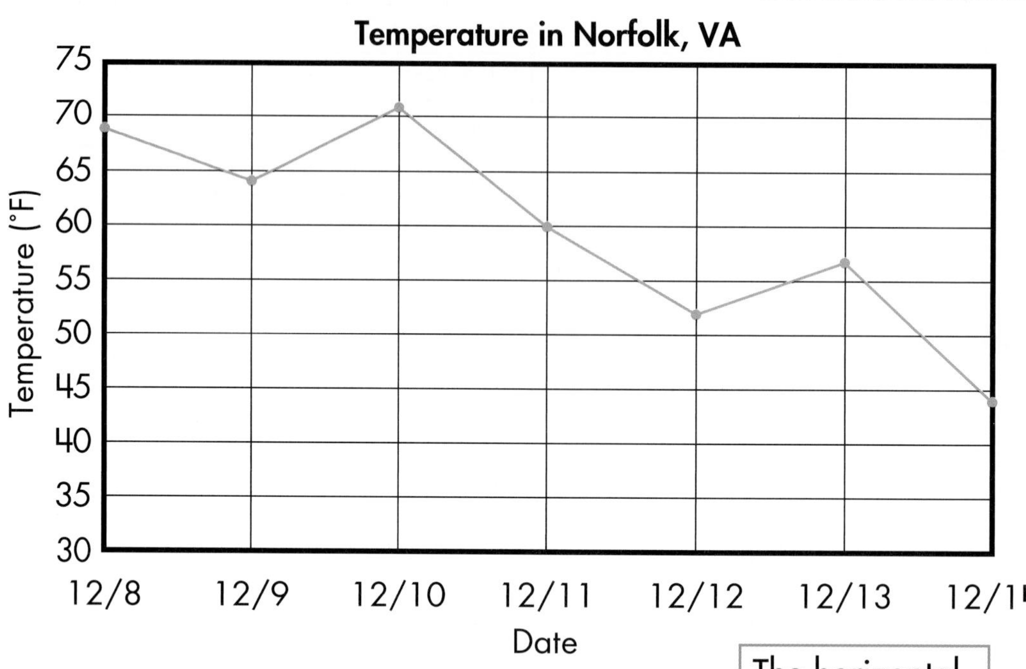

The horizontal axis or *x*-axis shows the date.

The graph was made from data collected and organized in this table.

DATE	TEMPERATURE
12/8	69° F
12/9	64° F
12/10	71° F
12/11	60° F
12/12	52° F
12/13	57° F
12/14	44° F

This row of the table shows that on December 11, the temperature was 60° F.

Reading Points on a Graph

(page 1 of 2)

Each point on this graph tells us two connected pieces of information, the date and the temperature.

For example, look at the point marked with a star ★ on the graph.

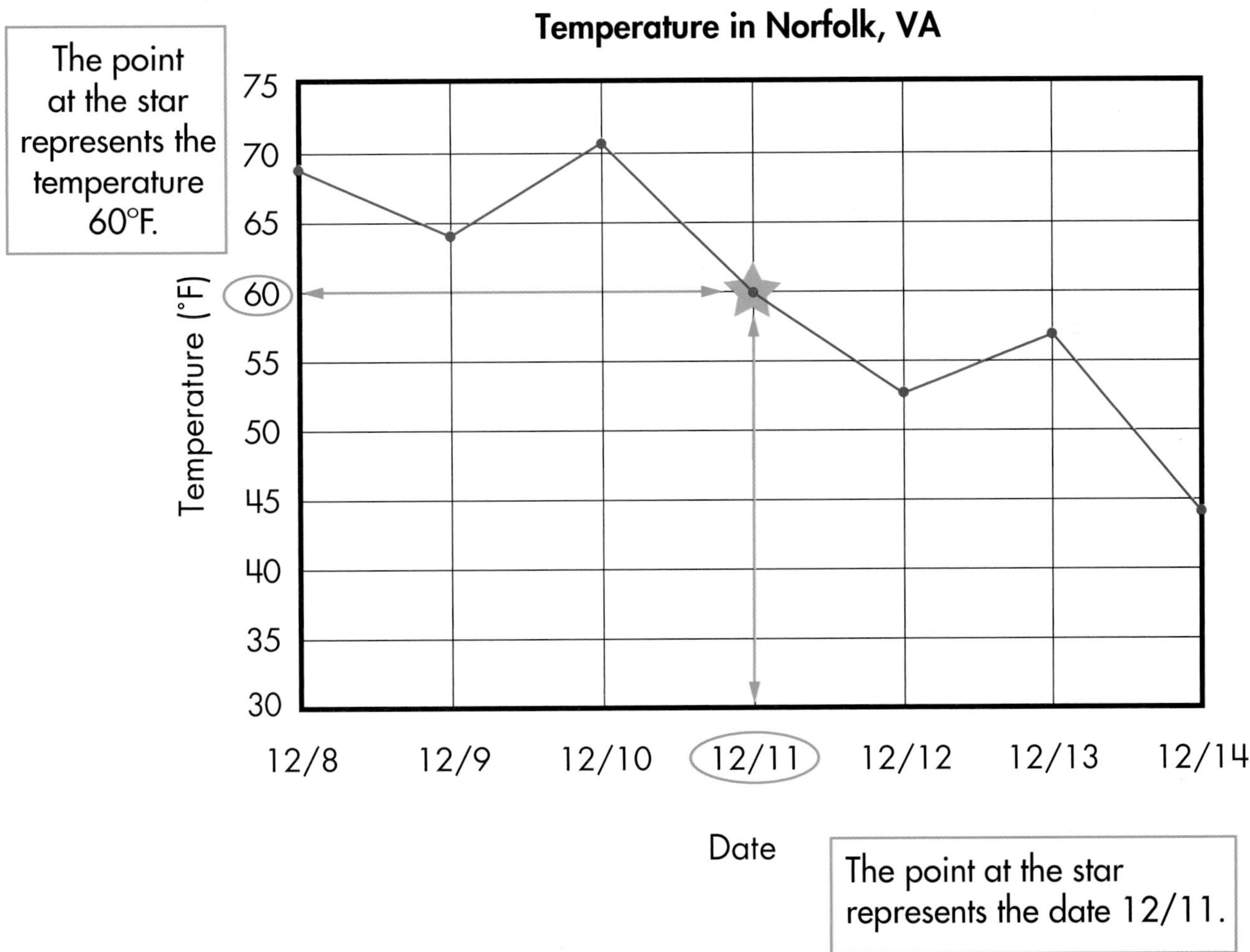

Putting those two pieces of information together, the point marked with a star ★ shows that on December 11 the temperature was 60°F in Norfolk, VA.

Reading Points on a Graph

(page 2 of 2)

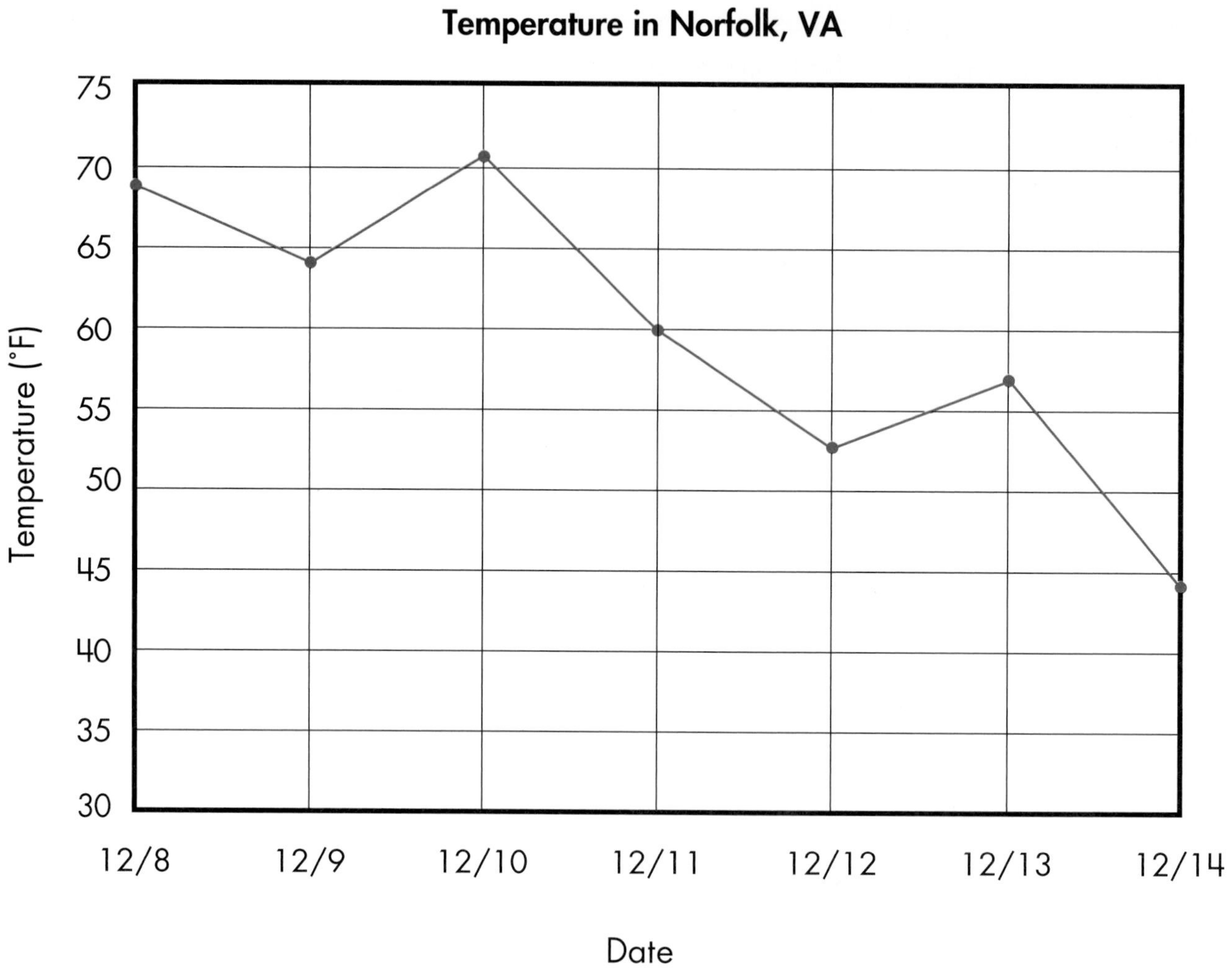

Temperature (°F)

75
70
65
60
55
50
45
40
35
30

12/8 12/9 12/10 12/11 12/12 12/13 12/14

Date

Answer these questions about the Norfolk temperature graph.

On which day was it the hottest?

What was the coldest temperature?

What was the difference between the hottest temperature and the coldest temperature?

Make a prediction: What do you think the temperature will be in Norfolk, VA, for December 15 and the next several days?

Telling Stories from Line Graphs (page 1 of 2)

Each of these line graphs represents part of a bicycle race.
The graphs show the speed of the cyclist.

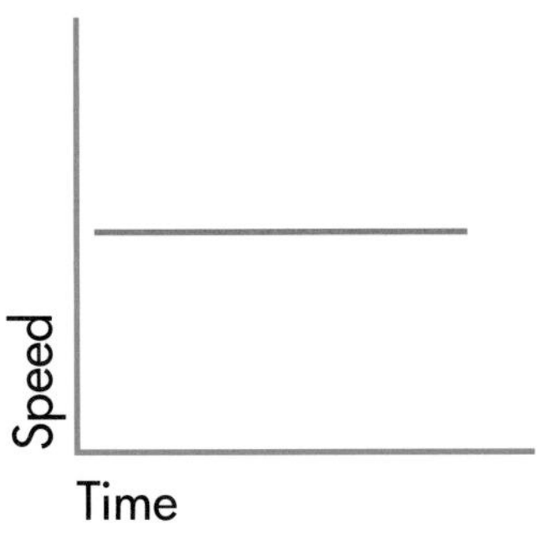

The speed is steady.

The cyclist rode at a constant speed.

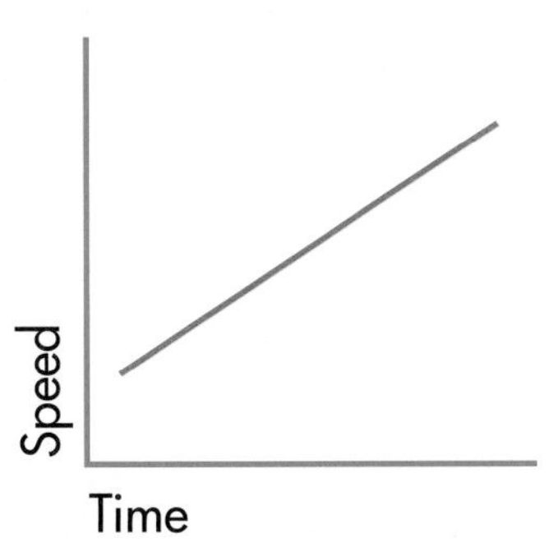

The speed is increasing.

The cyclist sped up to pass another rider.

The speed is decreasing.

The cyclist slowed down after she crossed the finish line.

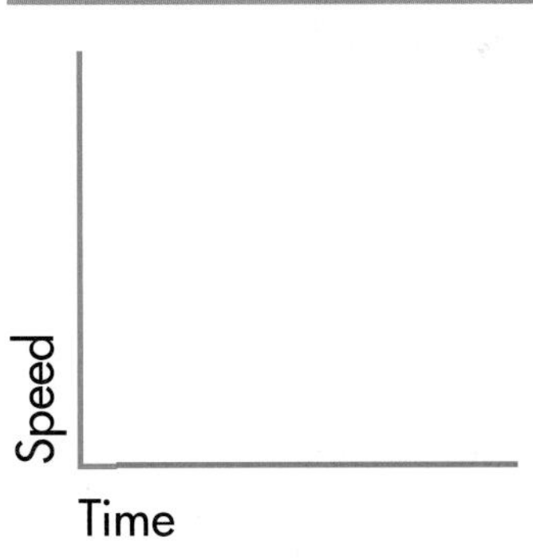

The speed is zero.

The cyclist stopped to receive her medal.

Telling Stories from Line Graphs (page 2 of 2)

Here is a graph that represents a complete bicycle race.

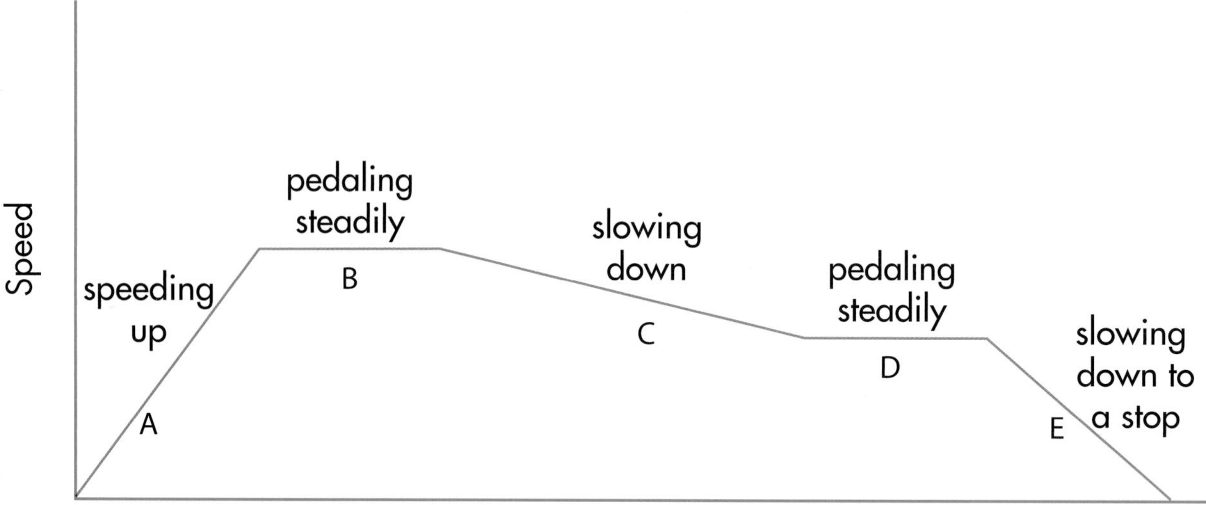

Jake wrote this story about the bicycle race.

At the start of the race, the cyclist sped up to her fastest speed. She pedaled steadily at that speed for a while, and then she slowed down. She pedaled steadily at the slower speed for a while. Then she slowed down and stopped at the end of the race.

Where on the graph is the cyclist's fastest speed?

Look at part B and part D on this graph. What is similar about these parts of the race? What is different?

How many times did the cyclist stop during the bicycle race? How do you know?

Fast and Slow Growth

These line graphs show how the heights of two different vegetable plants changed over one week.

The heights of both plants increased over the week, but the plants grew at different rates.

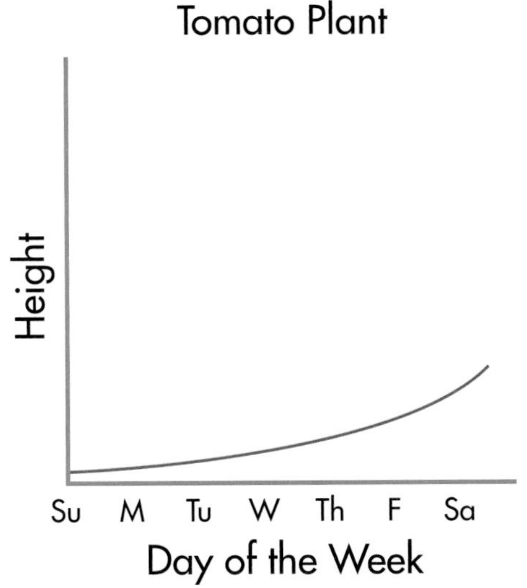

The tomato plant grew more slowly than the cucumber plant.

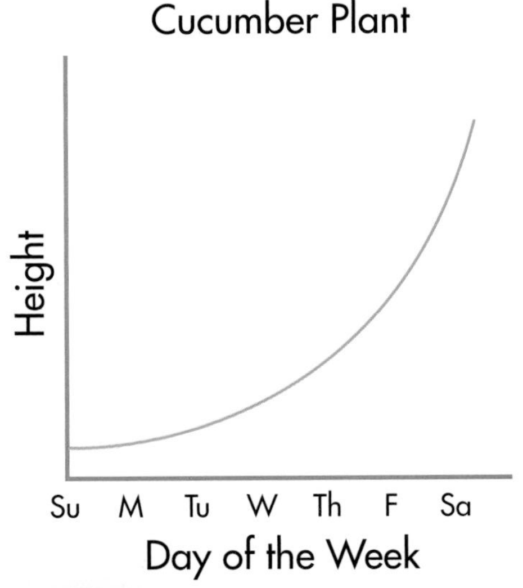

The cucumber plant grew more quickly than the tomato plant.

This graph shows the height of a green bean plant as it grew. Describe the rate of growth of the bean plant over the week.

Green Bean Plant

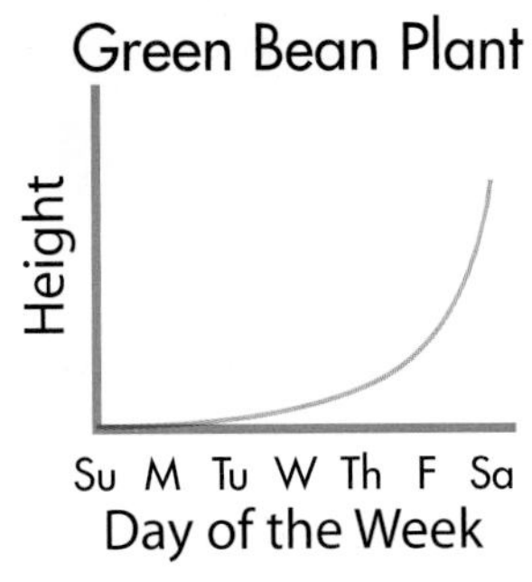

The Penny Jar and a Constant Rate of Change

Math Words
- **constant rate**

In some situations, change happens at a constant rate.

The Penny Jar problems in this unit are situations with a constant rate of change.

The rule for the Penny Jar shown below is:

Start with 3 pennies and add 5 pennies each round.

START

Total:
3 pennies

Round 1

Total:
8 pennies

Round 2

Total:
13 pennies

Round 5

Total:
28 pennies

The rate of change is constant.

The same amount, 5 pennies, is added in each round.

How Many Pennies in the Penny Jar?

For the Penny Jar on page 78, how many pennies will be in the jar after the 4th round?

Jill's solution

Jill drew a picture to find out.

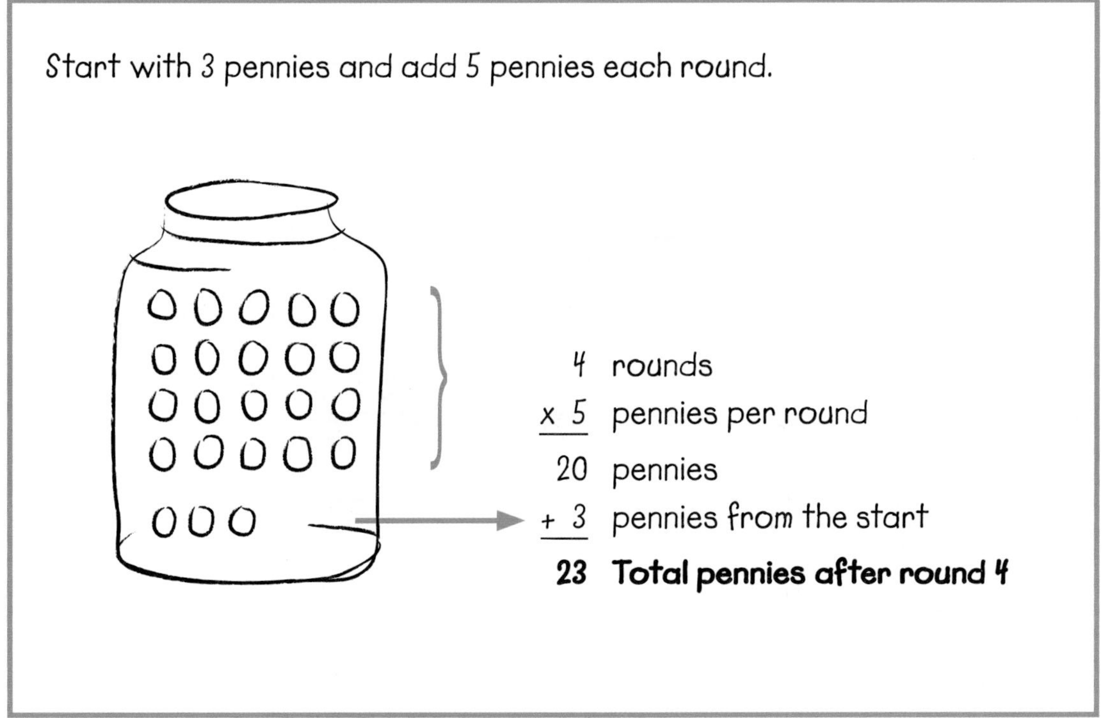

Start with 3 pennies and add 5 pennies each round.
4 rounds
x 5 pennies per round
20 pennies
+ 3 pennies from the start
23 Total pennies after round 4

How many pennies will be in the jar after the 6th round?
How many pennies will be in the jar after the 10th round?

A Table for a Penny Jar Problem

Anna made a table for this Penny Jar problem.

Start with 3 pennies and add 5 pennies each round.

Number of Rounds	Total Number of Pennies
Start	3
1	8
2	13
3	18
4	23
5	28
6	33
7	38
10	53
15	78
20	?

+ 5 each round

This row shows that after the 4th round there is a total of 23 pennies in the jar.

Beginning here the table skips some rows.

What is the total number of pennies for round 20? How did you figure that out?

A Graph for a Penny Jar Problem

Marisol made a graph for this Penny Jar problem.

Start with 3 pennies and add 5 pennies each round.

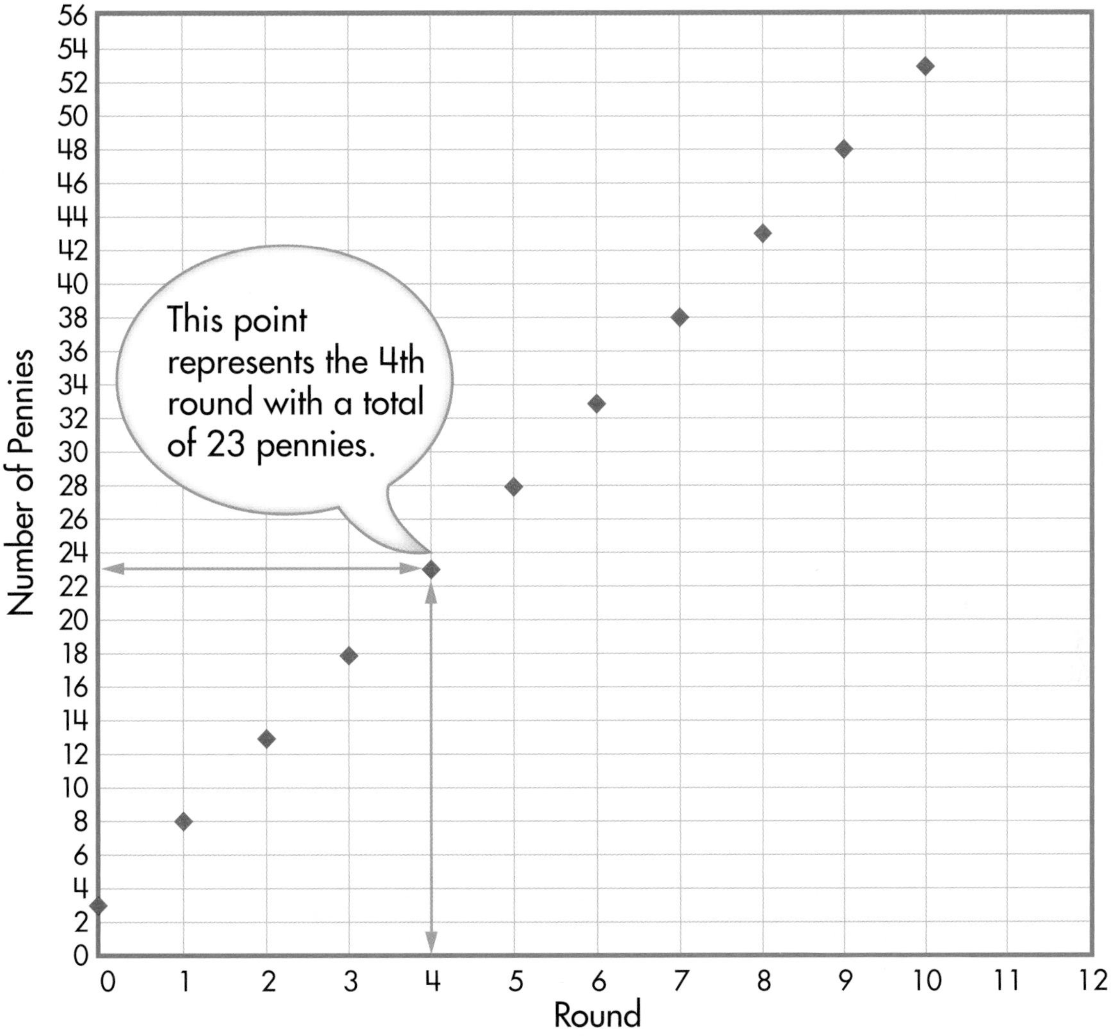

Number of Pennies: 0, 2, 4, 6, 8, 10, 12, 14, 16, 18, 20, 22, 24, 26, 28, 30, 32, 34, 36, 38, 40, 42, 44, 46, 48, 50, 52, 54, 56

Round: 0, 1, 2, 3, 4, 5, 6, 7, 8, 9, 10, 11, 12

This point represents the 4th round with a total of 23 pennies.

Marisol wondered, "Why are the points in a straight line?" Why do you think the points on the graph are in a straight line?

Penny Jar Comparisons

(page 1 of 4)

Here are two Penny Jar problems.

Penny Jar A
Start with 6 and add 4 each round.

Penny Jar B
Start with 0 and add 4 each round.

START

START

Will Penny Jar B ever have the same number of pennies as Penny Jar A?

First, Derek made a table.

Round	Penny Jar A	Penny Jar B
Start with	6	0
1	10	4
2	14	8
3	18	12
4	22	16
5	26	20
6	30	24

Penny Jar Comparisons

(page 2 of 4)

Next, Derek represented the table as a graph.

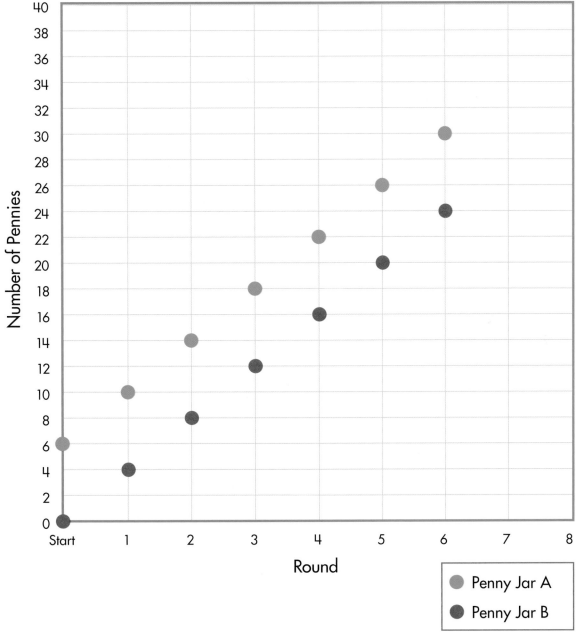

Number of Pennies

40
38
36
34
32
30
28
26
24
22
20
18
16
14
12
10
8
6
4
2
0

Start 1 2 3 4 5 6 7 8

Round

Penny Jar A
Penny Jar B

Will Penny Jar B ever have the same number of pennies as Penny Jar A? How does the table show that? How does the graph show that?

Penny Jar Comparisons

(page 3 of 4)

Here are two Penny Jar problems.

Penny Jar A

Start with 6 and add 4 each round.

Penny Jar C

Start with 4 and add 2 each round.

Will Penny Jar C ever have the same number of pennies as Penny Jar A?

Round	Penny Jar A	Penny Jar C
Start with	6	4
1	10	6
2	14	8
3	18	10
4	22	12
5	26	14
6	30	16

Neomi used a table and a graph to find out.

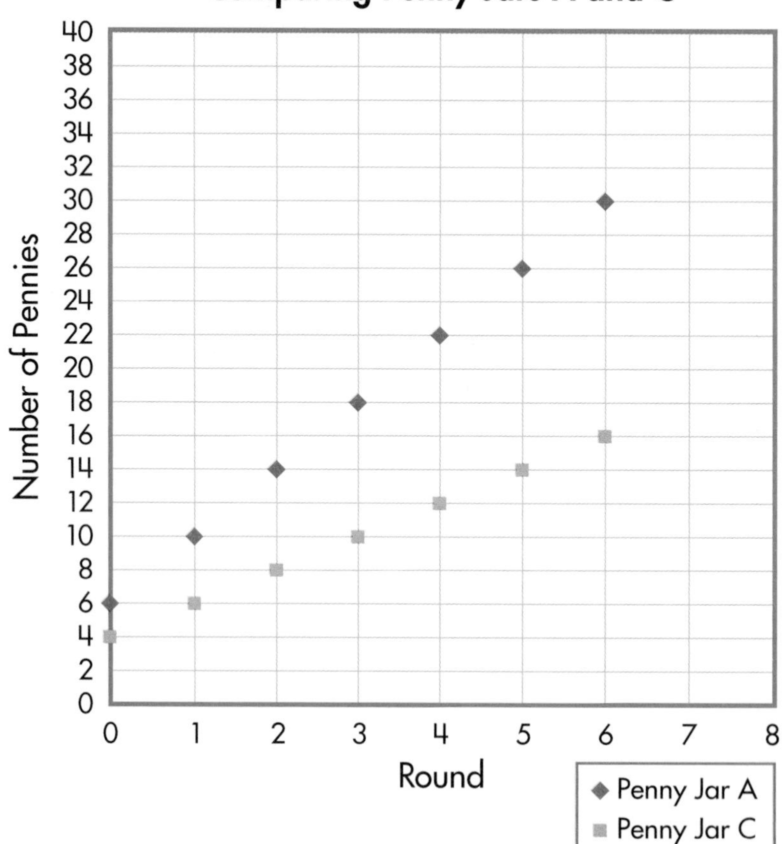

Will Penny Jar C ever have the same number of pennies as Penny Jar A? How does the table show that? How does the graph show that?

Penny Jar Comparisons

(page 4 of 4)

Here are two Penny Jar problems.

Penny Jar A
Start with 6 and add 4 each round.

Penny Jar D
Start with 0 and add 6 each round.

Will Penny Jar D ever have the same number of pennies as Penny Jar A?

Steve used a table and a graph to find out.

Round	Penny Jar A	Penny Jar D
Start with	6	0
1	10	6
2	14	12
3	18	18
4	22	24
5	26	30
6	30	36

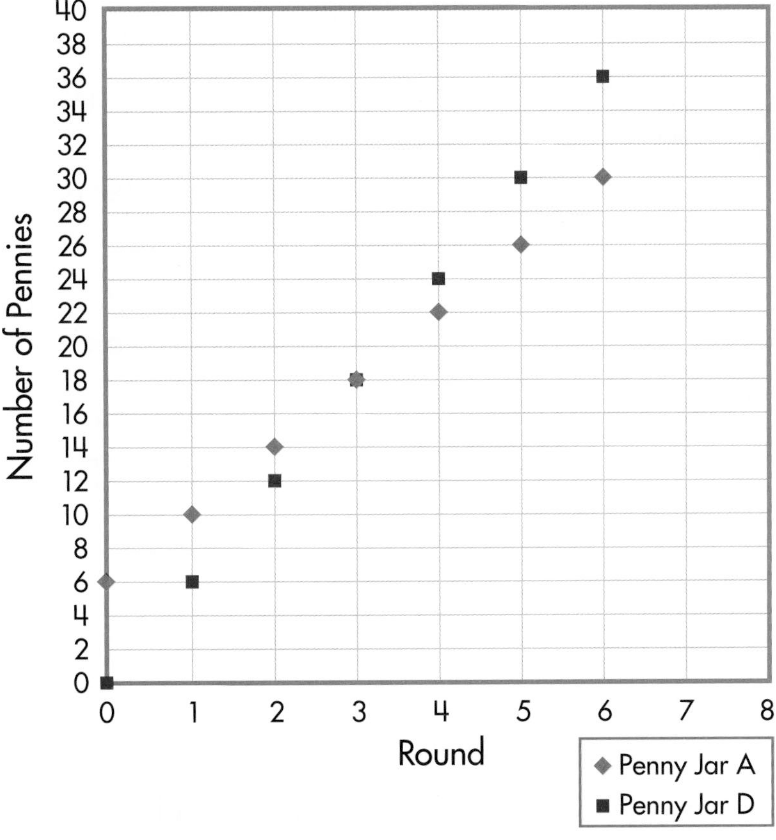

Will Penny Jar D ever have the same number of pennies as Penny Jar A? How does the table show that? How does the graph show that?

Writing Rules to Describe Change

Start with 8 pennies and add 5 pennies each round.

How many pennies will there be in the jar after 10 rounds?

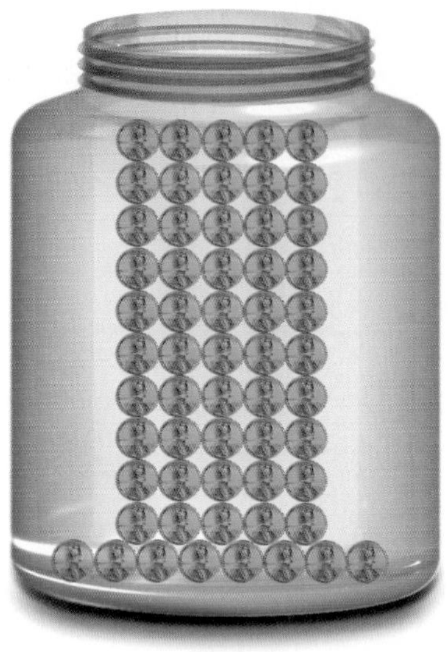

10	rounds
× 5	pennies per round
50	pennies
+ 8	pennies from the start
58	**Total pennies after round 10**

A teacher asked her students to write a rule for the number of pennies for any round, using words or an arithmetic expression.

Luke's rule: *You multiply the round number by 5, and then you add 8 because that is the number of pennies in the jar at the beginning.*

Steve's rule: *Round number x 5 + 8*

Sabrina's rule: $8 + (5 \times n)$

Can you use one of these rules or your own rule to find out how many pennies will be in the jar after round 30?

Is there ever a round when you will have exactly 200 pennies in this jar? (If so, what round will that be?) How do you know?

Working with Data

Math Words
- **data**

People collect data to gather information they want to know about the world around them.

By collecting, representing, and analyzing data, you can answer questions such as:

How many books do fourth graders read each month?

How much taller are fourth graders than first graders?

How long have our families lived in this town?

Which group watches more television per day, adults or children?

Working with data is a process.

Ask a question → Collect data → Organize and represent the data → Describe and summarize the data → Interpret the data, make conclusions, and ask new questions → (back to Ask a question)

Organizing and Representing Data

(page 1 of 2)

Math Words
• tally marks
• outlier
• median

Lucy wondered:

How many books do fourth graders read in one month?

She took a survey of her class and collected this set of data.

How many books did you read last month?			
Yuki 6	Amelia 7	Andreas 8	Anna 8
Lucy 11	Vashon 7	Ursula 8	Kaetwan 9
Enrique 10	Tairea 8	Ramona 10	Vanetta 10
Steve 9	Bill 8	Luke 15	Barney 9
Marisol 11	Duante 9	Emaan 10	Cheyenne 11
Laqueta 10	Derek 8		

Lucy decided to organize and represent the data in different ways.

First, she organized the data by using tally marks.

Number of books	Number of students
6	|
7	||
8	𝍸 |
9	||||
10	𝍸
11	|||
15	|

Organizing and Representing Data

(page 2 of 2)

Math Words
- **line plot**
- **bar graph**

Then Lucy represented the data in a line plot.

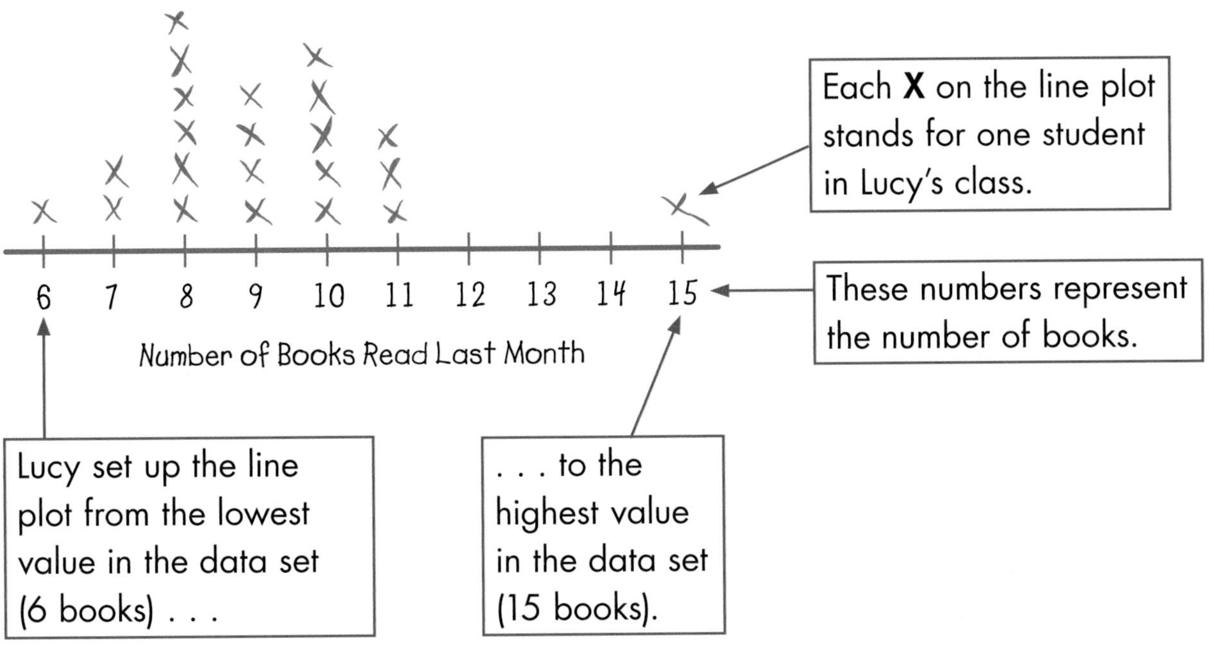
Each **X** on the line plot stands for one student in Lucy's class.
6 7 8 9 10 11 12 13 14 15
These numbers represent the number of books.
Number of Books Read Last Month
Lucy set up the line plot from the lowest value in the data set (6 books) . . .
. . . to the highest value in the data set (15 books).

She also represented the data in a bar graph.

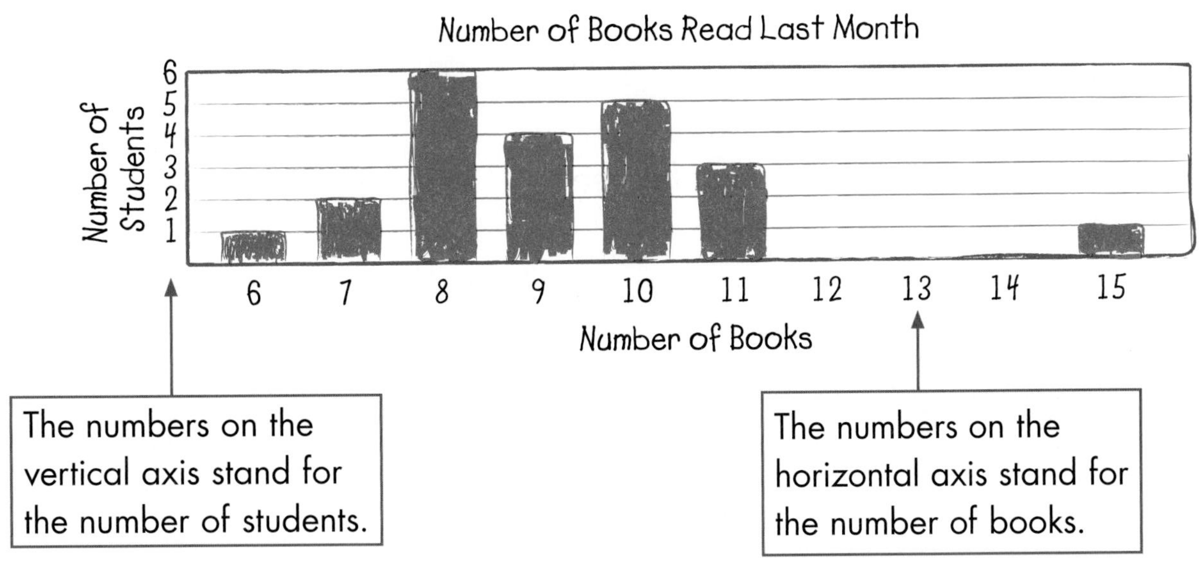
Number of Books Read Last Month
Number of Students
1 2 3 4 5 6
6 7 8 9 10 11 12 13 14 15
Number of Books
The numbers on the vertical axis stand for the number of students.
The numbers on the horizontal axis stand for the number of books.

Describing and Summarizing Data (page 1 of 2)

Math Words
- **range**
- **mode**

Lucy shared her data with her class.

The teacher asked, "What can you say about the number of books read by students in our class last month?"

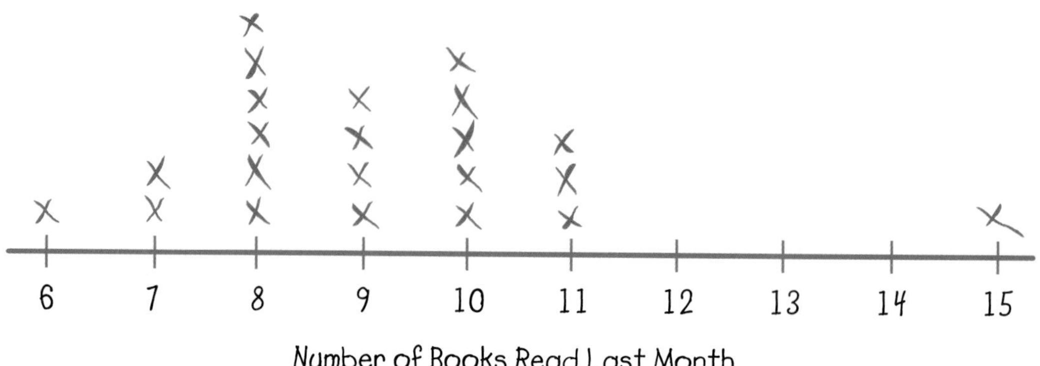

Here are some of the students' responses.

Luke noticed the range of this data set.

Luke: *The data range from 6 books to 15 books. No one in our class read fewer than 6 books and no one read more than 15 books.*

The **range** is the difference between the highest value and the lowest value in a set of data.

In this data, the range is 9 books.

15	−	6	=	9
highest value		lowest value		range

Tairea found an interval within which most of the data are concentrated.

Tairea: *More than half of the class read between 8 books and 10 books.*

Bill noticed the mode in this data set.

Bill: *More people read 8 books than any other number of books.*

The **mode** is the value that occurs most often in a set of data.

Describing and Summarizing Data (page 2 of 2)

Math Words
- **outlier**
- **median**

Barney noticed an outlier in this data set:

One person read 15 books and 15 books is far away from the rest of the data. Reading 15 books is unusual for our class, because most people read between 8 and 10 books.

An **outlier** is a piece of data that has an unusual value, much lower or much higher than most of the data.

Marisol found the median in this data set:

The median is 9 books. That means that half of the class read 9 books or more.

The **median** is the middle value of the data when all the data are put in order.

* Look for more information on the Math Words and Ideas page "Finding the Median."

Consider the outlier in Lucy's data.
What reasons could there be for one student reading 15 books?
What do you think the data show about this class?
If you were writing a newspaper article, what would you report?
What evidence from the data supports your ideas?

Finding the Median (page 1 of 2)

The median is the middle value of the data when all the data are put in order.

Look at these examples.

How many raisins are in a half-ounce box?

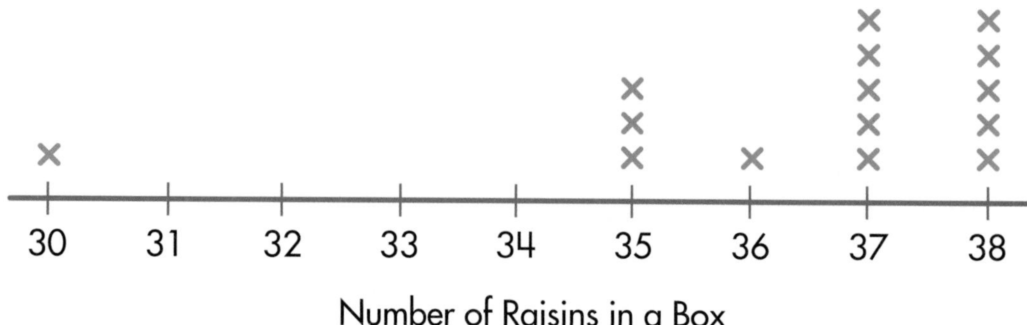

Here are all the data listed in order.

30, 35, 35, 35, 36, 37, 37, **37,** 37, 37, 38, 38, 38, 38, 38

median

The middle value is **37.**

The median value is **37 raisins.**

Half of the boxes had 37 raisins or fewer, and half of the boxes had 37 raisins or more.

Finding the Median (page 2 of 2)

When a set of data has an even number of values, the median is between the two middle values.

How many books did you read last summer?

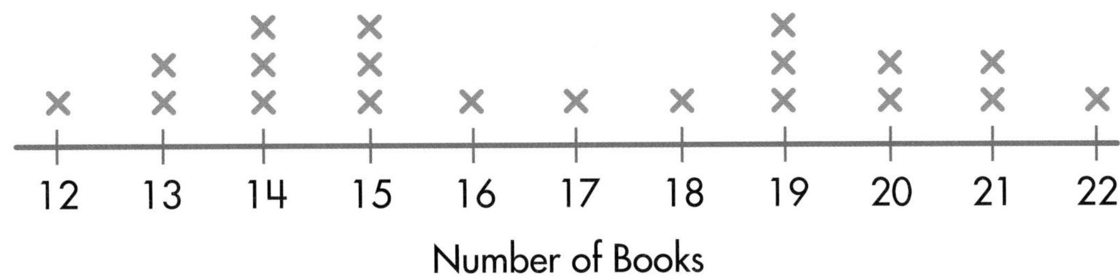

Here are all the data listed in order.

12, 13, 13, 14, 14, 14, 15, 15, 15, **16, 17,** 18, 19, 19, 19, 20, 20, 21, 21, 22

median

The middle values are not the same, so the median is midway between the two values 16 and 17. The median is **$16\frac{1}{2}$ books.**

There are as many students in the group who read $16\frac{1}{2}$ books or fewer as there are students who read $16\frac{1}{2}$ books or more.

Comparing Two Sets of Data (page 1 of 4)

Some of Lucy's classmates asked the following question:

How does the number of books read each month by fourth graders compare with the number of books read each month by seventh graders?

They collected data from a seventh grade class.

How many books did you read last month?

7	3	10	6	6	11	4
7	6	10	4	11	4	6
5	5	3	4	6	10	5

They organized the data from the seventh grade class by using tally marks.

Seventh Grade	
Number of books	Number of students
3	‖
4					
5				
6	~~||||~~
7	‖
10				
11	‖

Comparing Two Sets of Data (page 2 of 4)

Math Words
- **double bar graph**

Vashon, Duante, Cheyenne, and Yuki created representations to compare the data from the seventh-grade class with the data that Lucy collected from their fourth-grade class.

Vashon's representation

Vashon represented each set of data on a line plot:

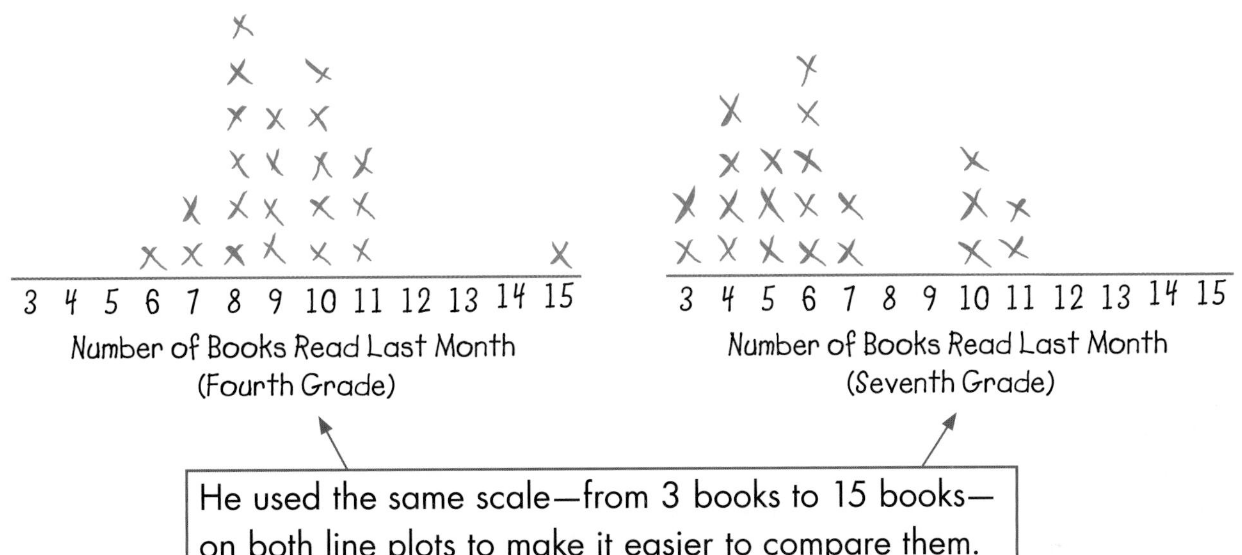

Cheyenne's representation

Cheyenne represented the data on a double bar graph.

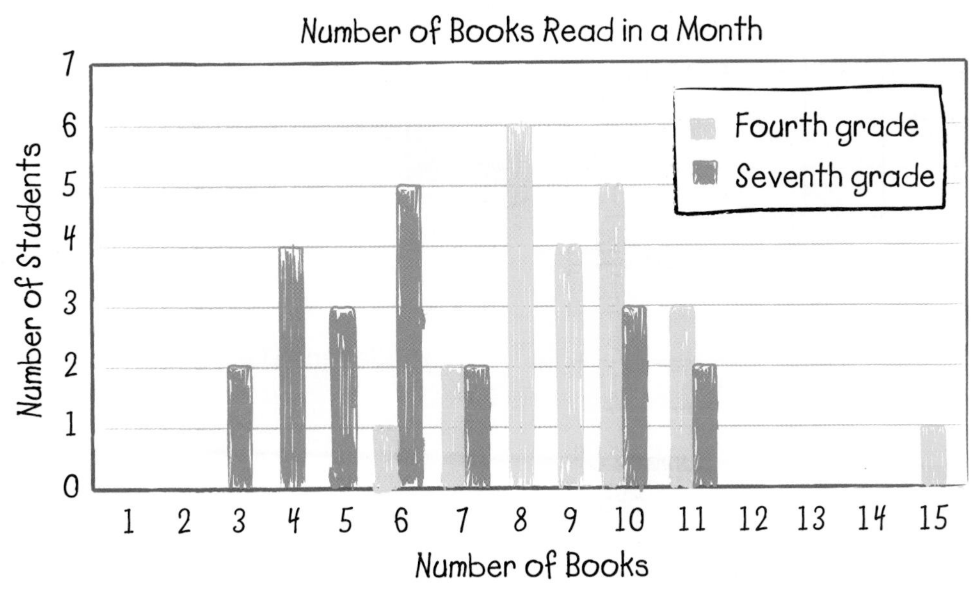

Comparing Two Sets of Data (page 3 of 4)

Duante's representation

Duante made a line plot and used the numbers 4 and 7 instead of **X**s to represent the students in the different grades.

							4					
							4					
			4		4		4					
			7		4		4	4				
	7		7	4	4	4	4	4				
	7	7	7	4	4	4	7	4				
7	7	7	7	7	4	4	7	7				
7	7	7	7	7	4	4	7	7				4
3	4	5	6	7	8	9	10	11	12	13	14	15

Number of Books Read Last Month by Fourth and Seventh Graders

Yuki's representation

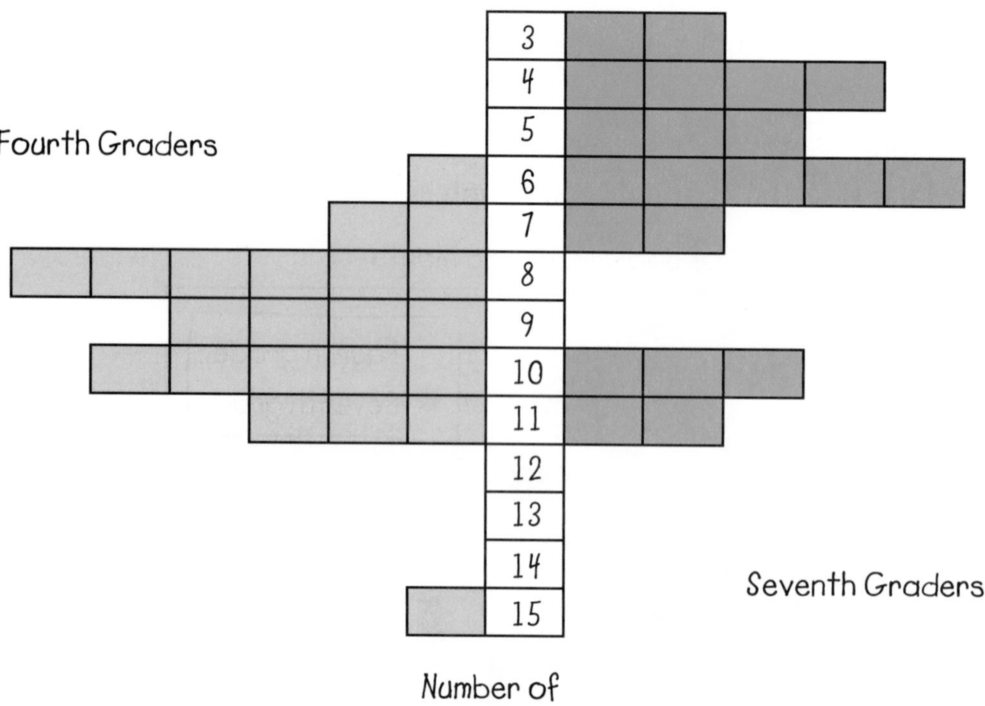

Comparing Two Sets of Data (page 4 of 4)

The students looked at their representations of the data they collected and compared the numbers of books read in one month by fourth graders and by seventh graders.

Here is what they noticed.

Vashon: *The lowest number of books a fourth grader read is 6 books. More than half of the seventh-grade students read 6 books or fewer.*

Duante: *The median in the seventh-grade data (6 books) is lower than the median in the fourth-grade data (9 books).*

Cheyenne: *The fourth-grade data are clustered mostly between 8 books and 10 books. Most of the seventh-grade data are clustered between 3 books and 7 books.*

Yuki: *One fourth grader read more books than any of the seventh graders.*

Based on what they noticed in the data they compared, Vashon, Duante, Cheyenne, and Yuki came to these conclusions:

Our data show that, overall, the fourth-grade students read more books than the seventh-grade students. The median value for seventh graders was lower than the median value for fourth graders. Even though one fourth grader read more books than anyone, that wasn't typical of all the fourth graders. More than half the seventh graders read 6 or fewer books, which is the lowest number read by a fourth grader.

Maybe the books that seventh graders read are longer than the books that fourth graders read. Maybe seventh graders have more homework than we do, and they don't have time to read. Maybe they don't have good books in their room like we do.

What new survey question could these students ask next to get more information about the reading habits of fourth and seventh graders?

Probability (page 1 of 3)

Math Words
- **probability**
- **impossible**
- **certain**

How likely is it . . . ? What are the chances . . . ?

Probability is the study of measuring how likely it is that something will happen. Sometimes we estimate probability on the basis of data and experience about how the world works.

Some future events are impossible, based on what we know about the world.

The entire Pacific Ocean will freeze this winter.

Some future events are certain.

The sun will rise tomorrow.

The probability of many other events falls between impossible and certain.

No one in our class will be absent tomorrow.

It will rain next weekend.

Likelihood Line

Impossible — A — Maybe — B — Certain

Can you think of events that can go at points A and B on the likelihood line?

Probability (page 2 of 3)

In some situations, there is a certain number of equally likely outcomes. In these situations, you can find the probability of an event by looking at how many different ways it can turn out.

What will happen if you toss a coin?

There are two possible outcomes. You can get heads or tails. If the coin is fair, there is a 1 out of 2 chance that you will get heads and a 1 out of 2 chance that you will get tails.

What can happen if you roll a number cube marked with the numbers 1, 2, 3, 4, 5, and 6?

There are six possible outcomes. If the number cube is fair, every number is just as likely to come up as any other number.

The probability of getting a five is 1 out of 6.

What is the chance of rolling an even number?

1	2
3	4
5	6

There are 3 even numbers out of 6 possibilities. So, there is a 3 out of 6 chance of rolling an even number.

You can also say that this is a 1 out of 2 chance.

What can happen if you pull a marble out of a jar that contains 3 yellow marbles and 9 blue marbles?

There are 12 marbles in the jar. The chance of pulling out a blue marble is 9 out of 12.

You can also say this is a 3 out of 4 chance.

Probability (page 3 of 3)

In mathematics, you can use numbers from 0 to 1 to describe the probability of an event.

The probability of an impossible event is 0.

The probability of a certain event is 1.

The probability of an event that is equally likely to happen or not happen is $\frac{1}{2}$.

For example, when you flip a fair coin there there is a 1 out of 2 chance that you will get heads. The probability of getting heads is $\frac{1}{2}$.

Probabilities can fall anywhere from 0 to 1.

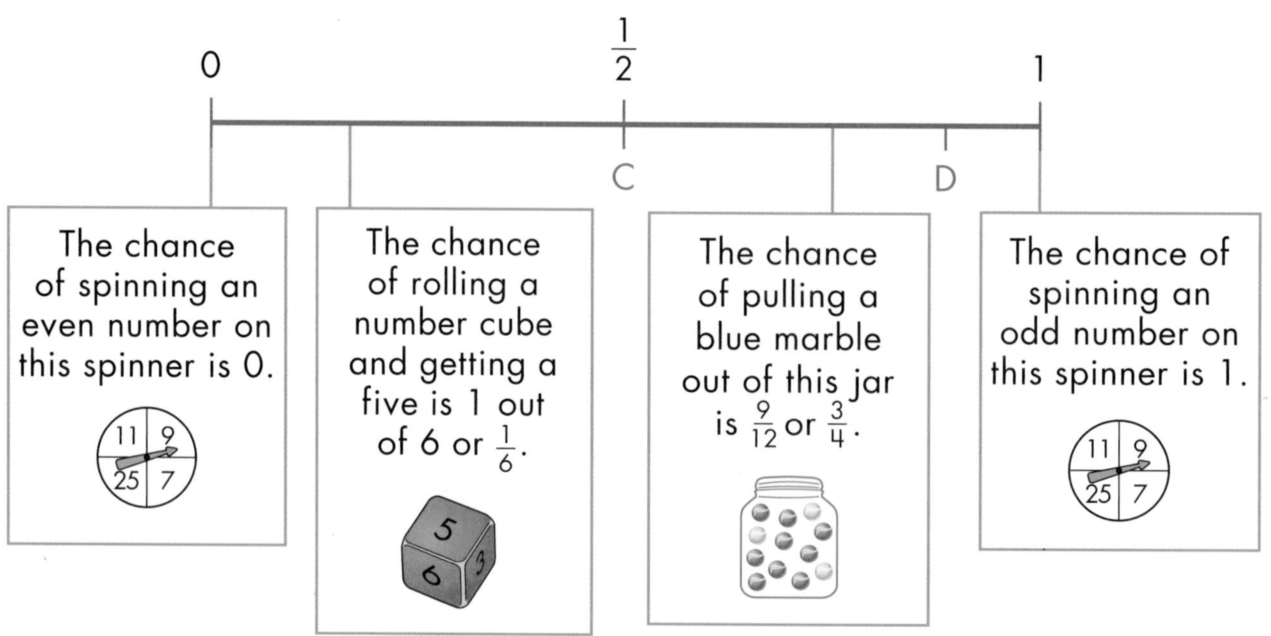

0
1/2
1
C
D
The chance of spinning an even number on this spinner is 0.
11 9 25 7
The chance of rolling a number cube and getting a five is 1 out of 6 or 1/6.
5 6 3
The chance of pulling a blue marble out of this jar is 9/12 or 3/4.
The chance of spinning an odd number on this spinner is 1.
11 9 25 7

Describe events that can go at points C and D on the line. You can use the idea of a spinner, a number cube, or pulling marbles out of a jar.

Linear Measurement (page 1 of 2)

By measuring length you can answer questions such as the following:

How wide is this window? 	How long is the balance beam? 

A ruler is a tool to measure length.

Most rulers measure inches on one edge and centimeters on the other edge.

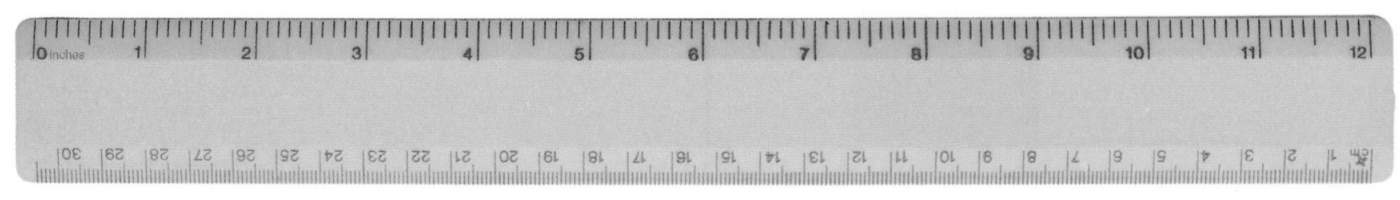

A ruler is 12 inches (or 1 foot) long. It is about $30\frac{1}{2}$ centimeters long.

Here are some other measuring tools.

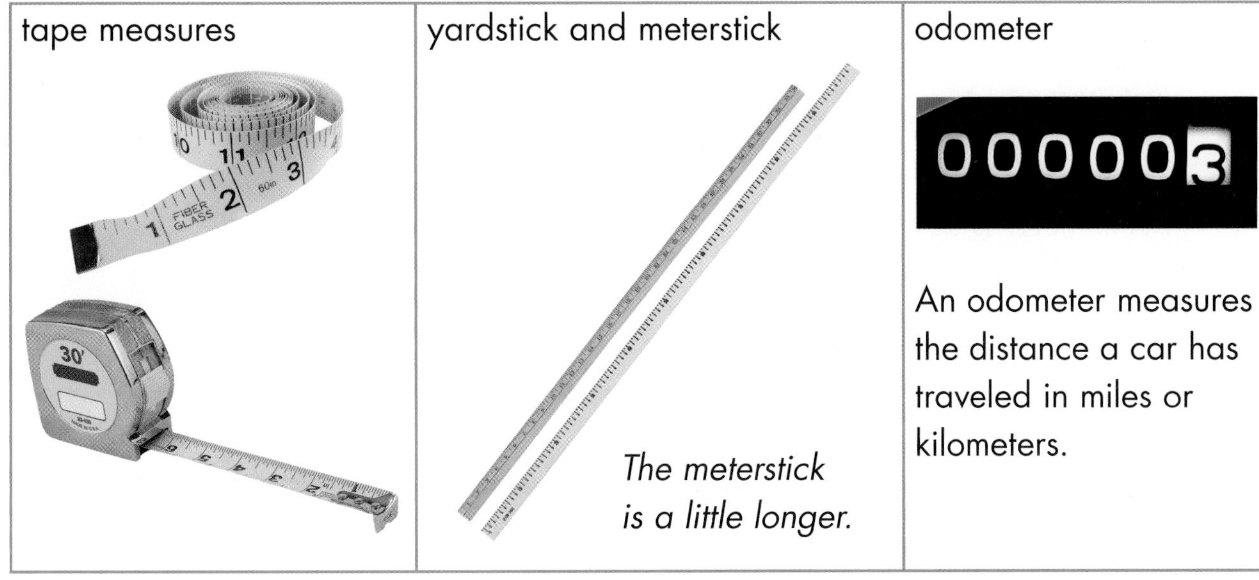

tape measures	yardstick and meterstick	odometer
	The meterstick is a little longer.	An odometer measures the distance a car has traveled in miles or kilometers.

Linear Measurement (page 2 of 2)

There are two different systems of measuring length.

People in the United States use the U.S. standard system to measure most lengths, using inches, feet, yards, and miles. Only two other countries in the world—Liberia and Myanmar—use this measurement system.

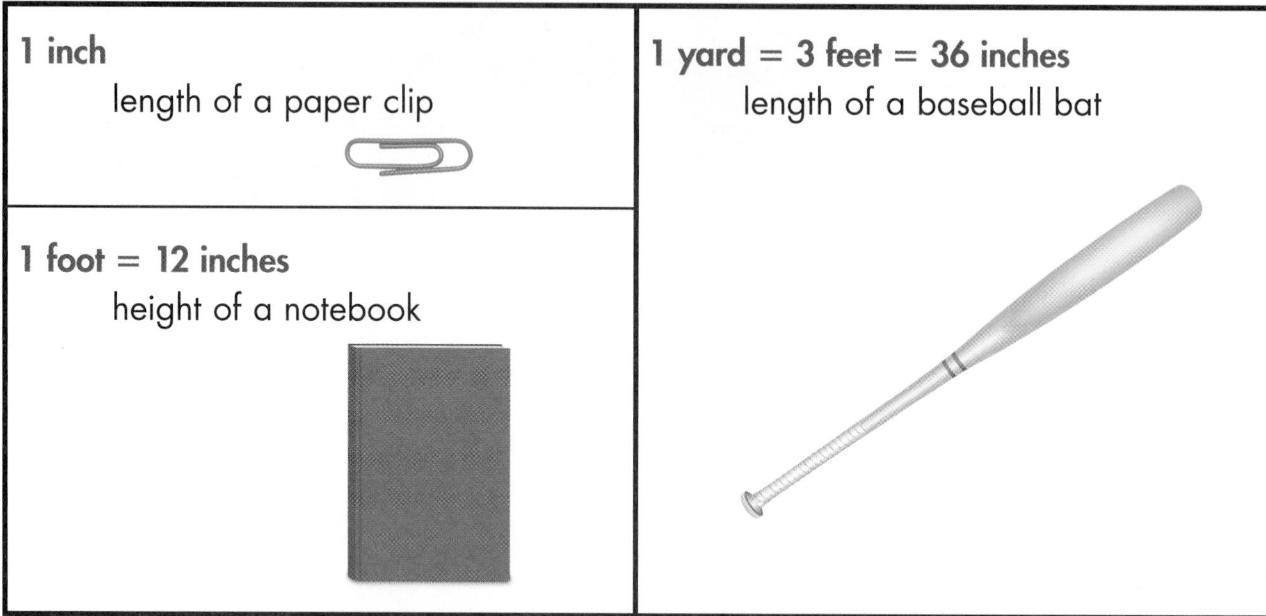

1 inch
length of a paper clip

1 foot = 12 inches
height of a notebook

1 yard = 3 feet = 36 inches
length of a baseball bat

People from most other countries around the world use the metric system for measuring lengths, using millimeters, centimeters, meters, and kilometers.

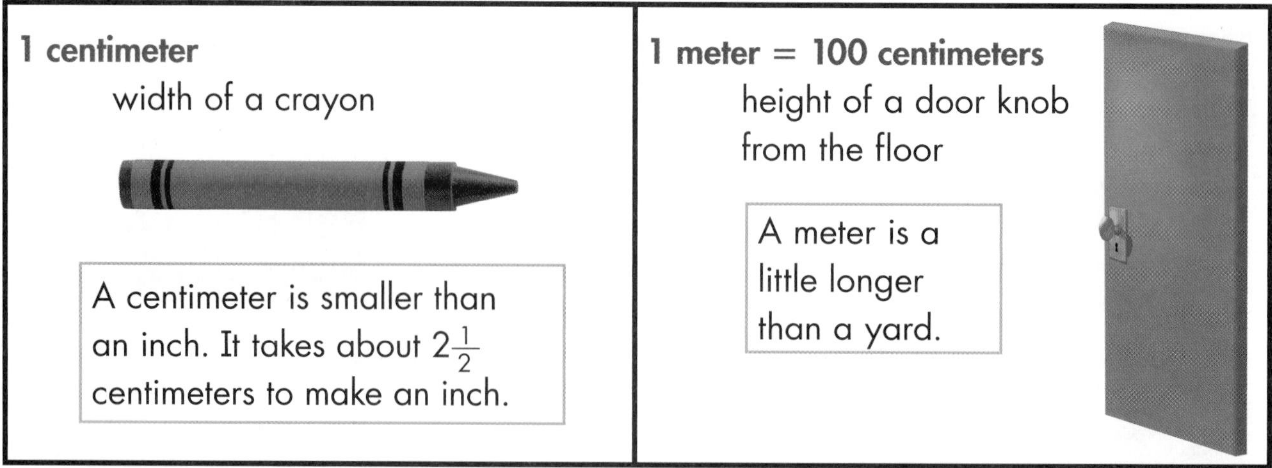

1 centimeter
width of a crayon

A centimeter is smaller than an inch. It takes about $2\frac{1}{2}$ centimeters to make an inch.

1 meter = 100 centimeters
height of a door knob from the floor

A meter is a little longer than a yard.

Can you find some other things that are about the length of an inch, a foot, a yard, a centimeter, or a meter?

Measuring Accurately

The students in Ms. Smith's class used rulers to measure the length of the chalkboard tray in their classroom. Even though the students measured the same distance, they got several different answers.

Look at the pictures below and look for the measurement mistakes the students made.

Jill measured 3 feet.

Jill: *I left gaps between the rulers, so my answer is too small.*

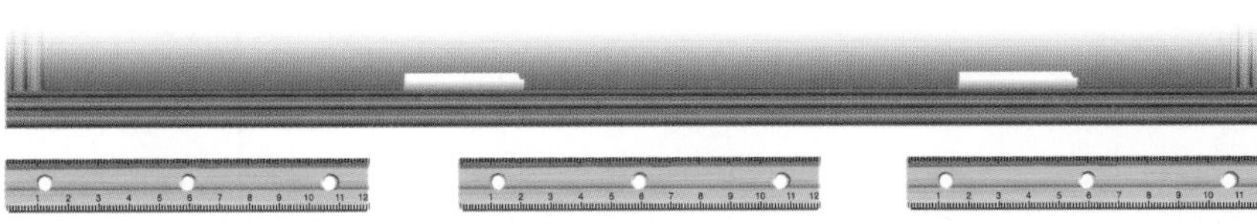

Andreas measured 4 feet.

Andreas: *I overlapped the rulers, so my answer is too big.*

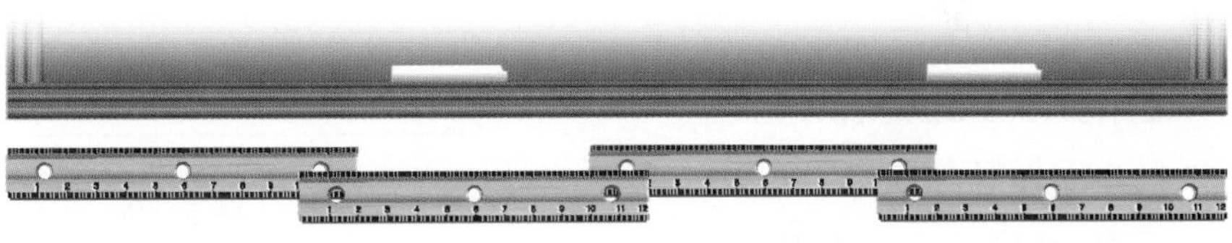

Yuson measured 3 feet.

Yuson: *I didn't start measuring at the beginning of the chalk tray and I didn't measure all the way to the end.*

Terrell measured 4 feet.

Terrell: *I didn't keep the rulers straight.*

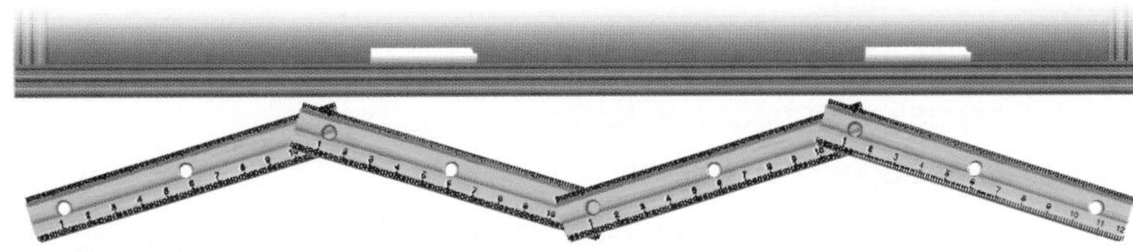

Tonya measured $3\frac{1}{2}$ feet.

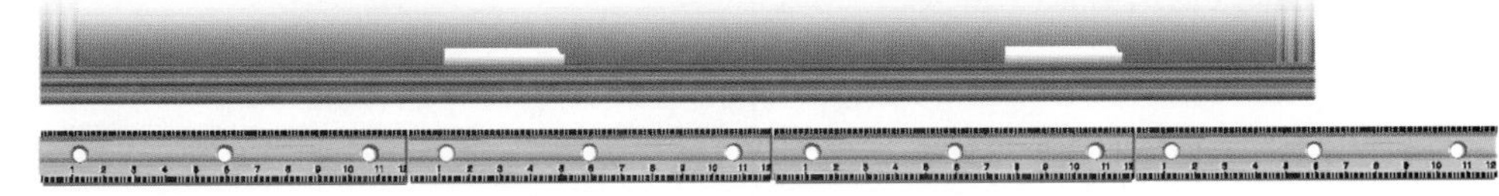

Tonya: *I lined up the ruler to the left side of the chalk tray. My rulers lined up exactly with no overlaps or gaps.*

Did Tonya measure the length of the chalk tray accurately? How do you know?

Perimeter (page 1 of 2)

Math Words
- **perimeter**

Perimeter is the length of the border of a figure. Perimeter is a linear measure.

An ant walks around the perimeter of the top of a desk by starting at one corner, walking all the way around the border, and ending at the same corner where it started.

How far did the ant walk?

What is the perimeter of the top of this desk?

Ramona's solution

I measured the sides of the desk by using feet.

$5 + 5 + 2\frac{1}{2} + 2\frac{1}{2} = 15$

The perimeter of the top of the desk is **15 feet.**

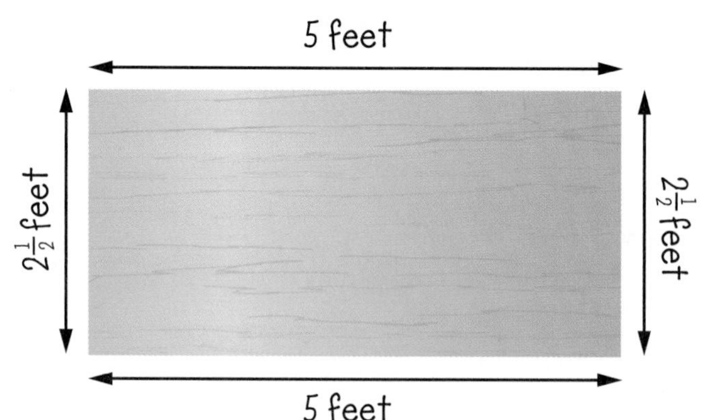

Luke's solution

I measured the sides of the desk by using inches. The left side measured 30 inches. The right side will measure the same as the left side.

The top measured 60 inches. The bottom will measure the same as the top.

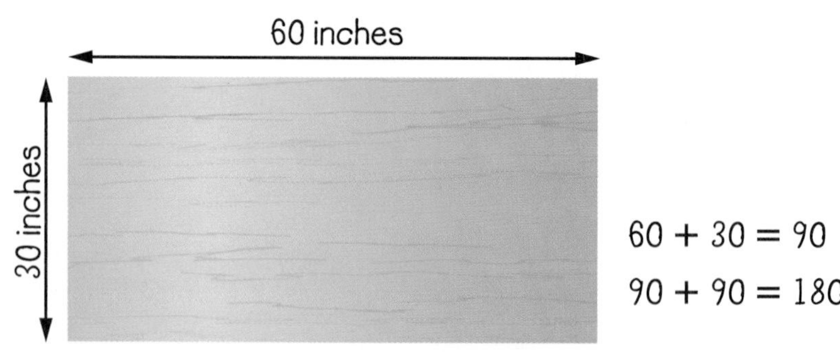

The perimeter of the top of the desk is **180 inches.**

Why is the answer in feet different from the answer in inches?

Perimeter (page 2 of 2)

Fill in the missing measures and find the perimeter.

Use the *LogoPaths* software to solve problems about perimeter.

Helena's solution

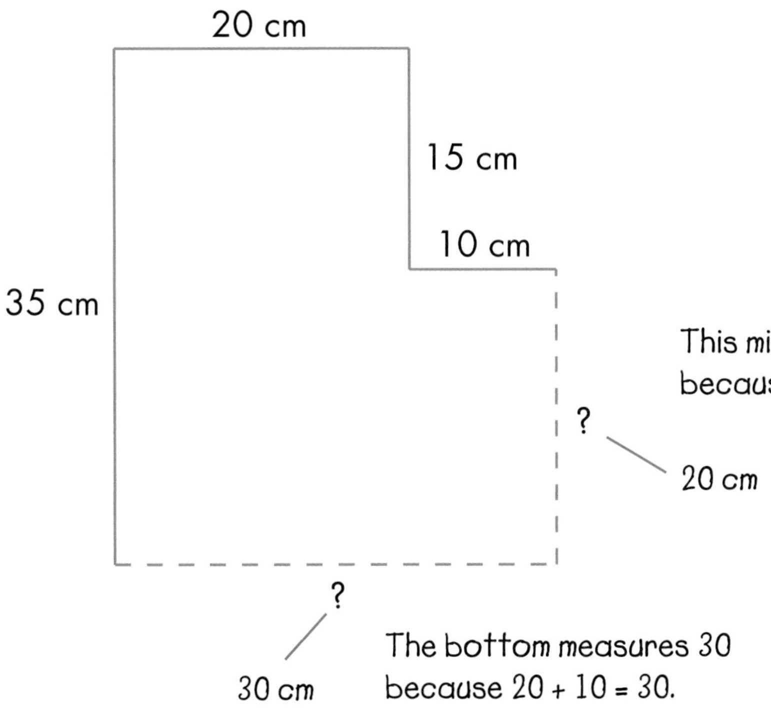

20 cm

15 cm

10 cm

35 cm

This missing part is 20 because 15 + 20 = 35.

?

20 cm

?

30 cm

The bottom measures 30 because 20 + 10 = 30.

35 + 20 + 15 + 10 + 20 + 30 = 130

The perimeter is **130 centimeters.**

Draw a rectangle with a perimeter of 600 meters.

Terrell's solution

If the perimeter is 600 meters, then halfway around is 300 meters.

The top and side measures of the rectangle must equal 300 meters, like 250 + 50.

250 meters

250 + 50 = 300

300 x 2 = 600

50 meters

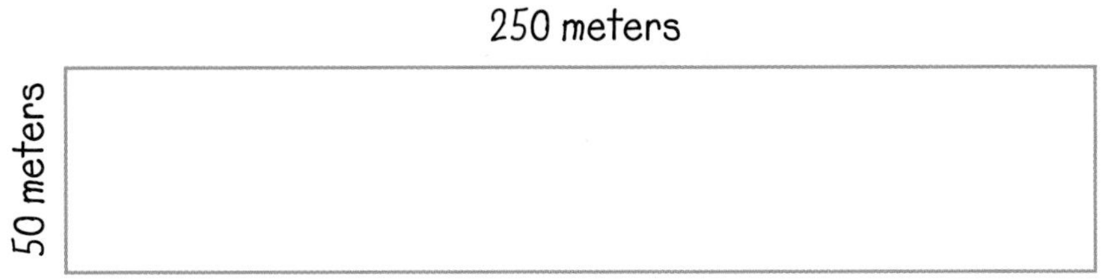

The perimeter of this rectangle is **600 meters.**

Polygons

Math Words
- **polygon**
- **two-dimensional (2-D)**

Polygons are closed two-dimensional (2-D) figures with straight sides.

These figures are polygons.

These figures are not polygons.

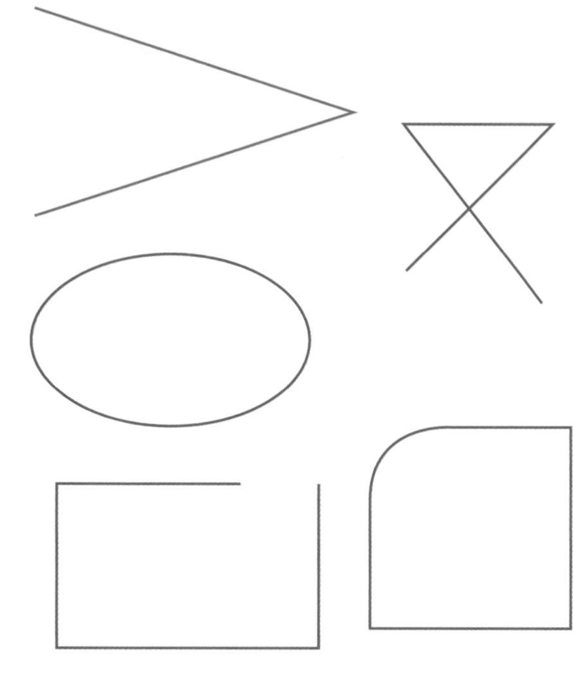

Which of these figures are polygons?

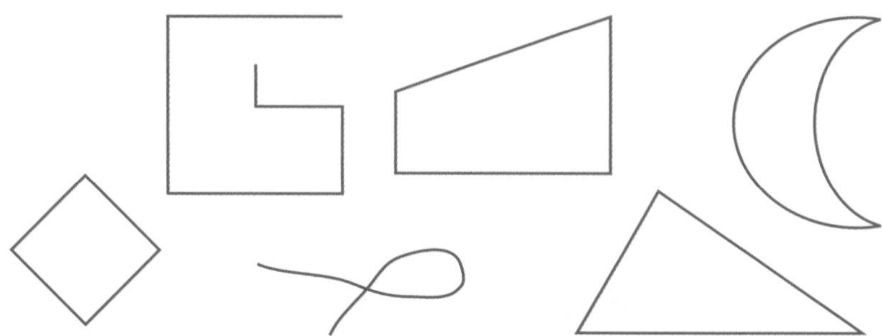

Naming Polygons

Polygons are named for the number of sides they have.

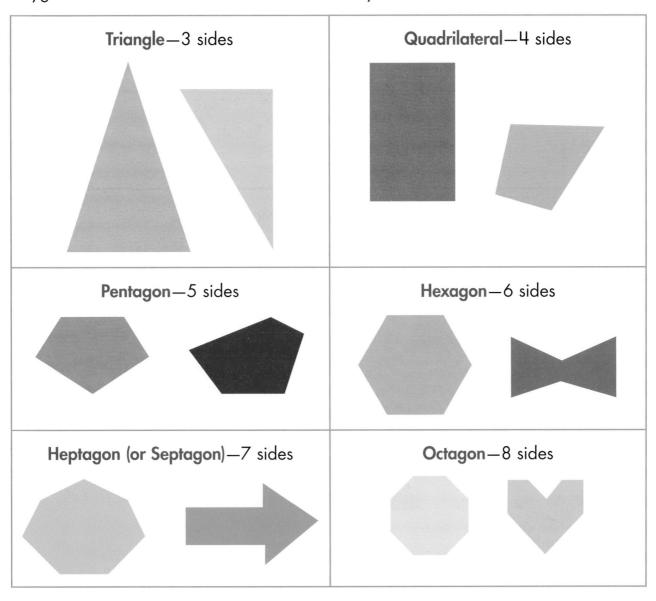

Triangle—3 sides	**Quadrilateral**—4 sides
Pentagon—5 sides	**Hexagon**—6 sides
Heptagon (or Septagon)—7 sides	**Octagon**—8 sides

Try drawing examples of the following polygons:
nonagon (9 sides)
decagon (10 sides)
hendecagon (11 sides)
dodecagon (12 sides)

Quadrilaterals (page 1 of 2)

Math Words
- **quadrilateral**
- **rhombus**

A quadrilateral is a polygon that has all of the following features:

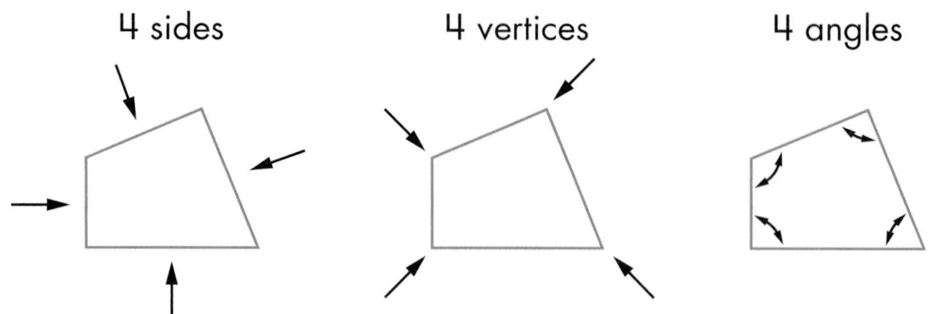
4 sides
4 vertices
4 angles

All of these figures are quadrilaterals. Some quadrilaterals have other special names, too.

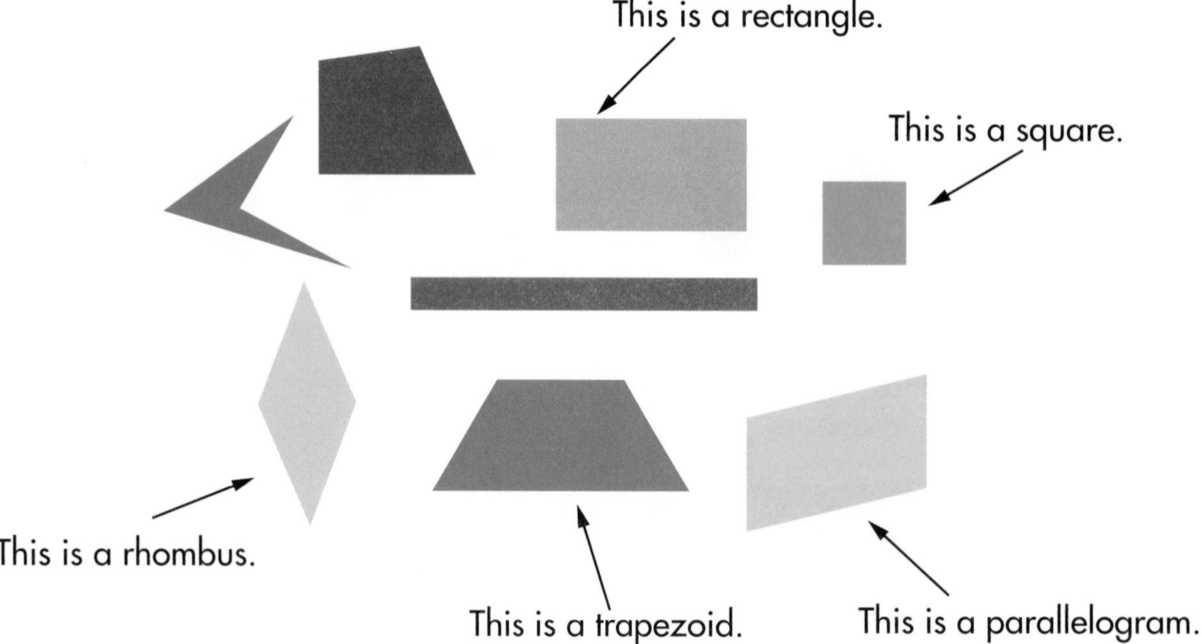
This is a rectangle.
This is a square.
This is a rhombus.
This is a trapezoid.
This is a parallelogram.

Which are quadrilaterals? Why do you think so?

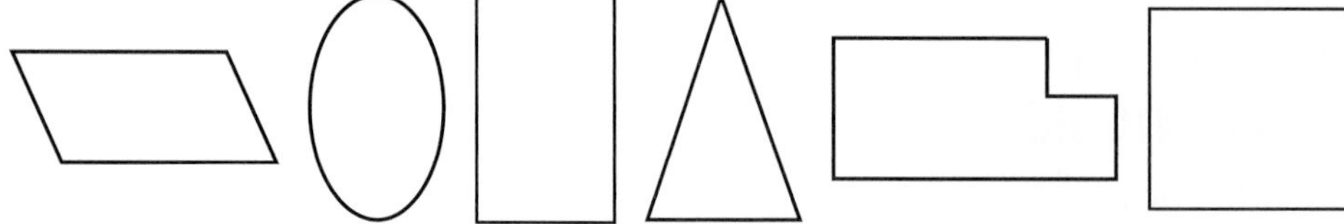

Quadrilaterals (page 2 of 2)

Math Words
- **parallel**
- **trapezoid**
- **parallelogram**

Parallel lines go in the same direction and are equidistant from each other, as railroad tracks do.

Quadrilaterals that have only 1 pair of parallel sides are called trapezoids.

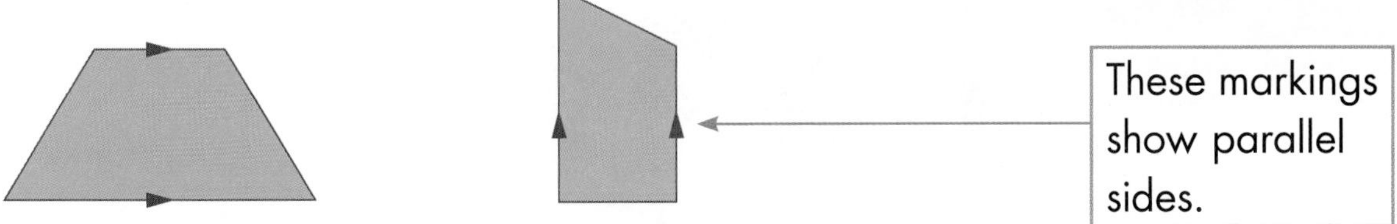
These markings show parallel sides.

Both of these quadrilaterals are trapezoids.

Quadrilaterals that have 2 pairs of parallel sides are called parallelograms.

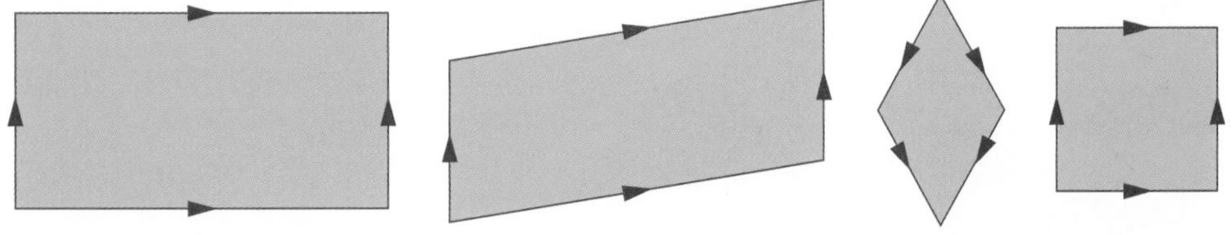

All of these quadrilaterals are parallelograms.

Some quadrilaterals have no parallel sides.

Rectangles and Squares

Math Words
- **rectangle**
- **square**

A rectangle is a special kind of quadrilateral that has the following features:

- 4 sides
- 4 vertices
- 4 angles that all measure 90° (right angles)

You can read more about right angles on page 111.

Here are some rectangles.

A square is a special kind of rectangle. It has the following features:

- 4 sides that are all the same length
- 4 vertices
- 4 angles that all measure 90° (right angles)

Here are some squares.

What is the same about rectangles and squares?
What is different about rectangles and squares?

Angles (page 1 of 3)

Math Words
- **angle**
- **degrees**
- **right angle**

The measure of an angle in a polygon is the amount of turn between two sides.

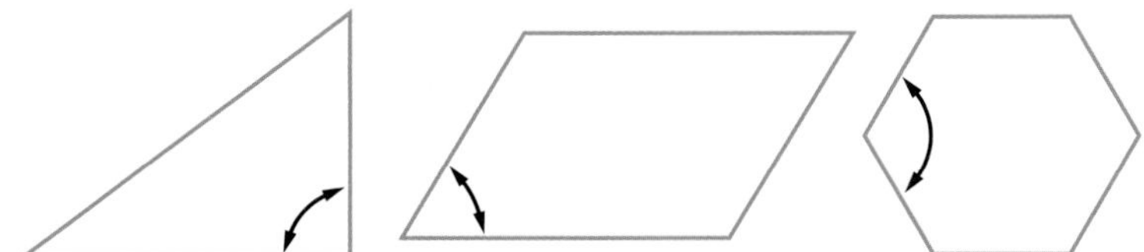

Angles are measured in degrees. When an angle makes a square corner, like the corner of a piece of paper, it is called a right angle. A right angle measures 90 degrees.

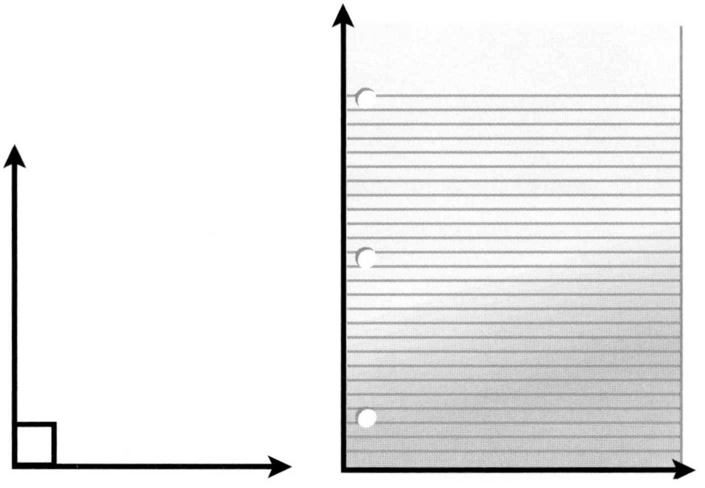

The word *"degree"* has another meaning, as a unit to measure temperature.

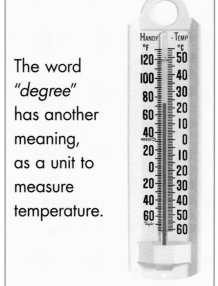

These students are talking about the angles in these polygons from their set of Power Polygons.

Enrique: *These triangles all have one 90-degree angle.*

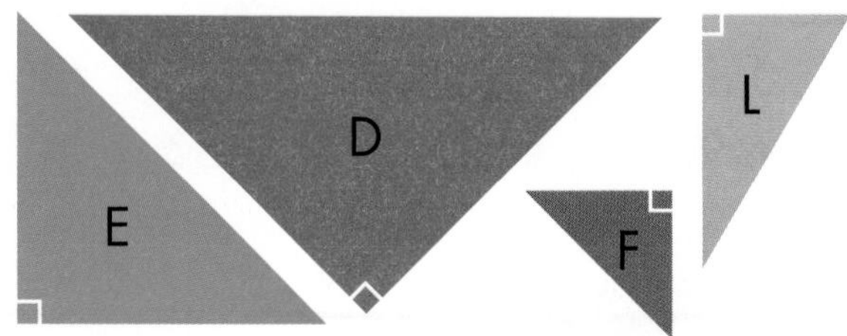

Amelia: *All of the angles in all of these rectangles are right angles.*

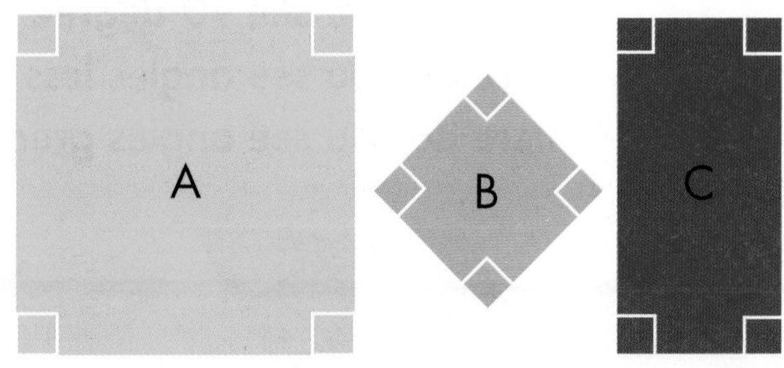

Angles (page 2 of 3)

Math Words
- **acute angle**
- **obtuse angle**

Helena: *None of the angles in this trapezoid measures 90 degrees.*

K

This angle is less than 90 degrees. It is smaller than the corner of the paper.

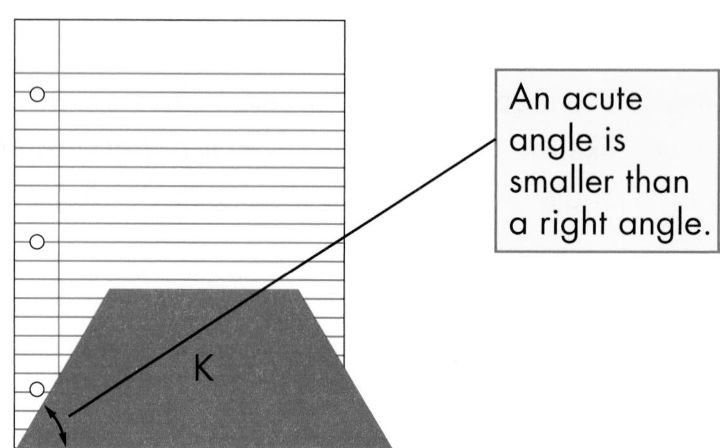
K
An acute angle is smaller than a right angle.

This angle is greater than 90 degrees. It is larger than the corner of the paper.

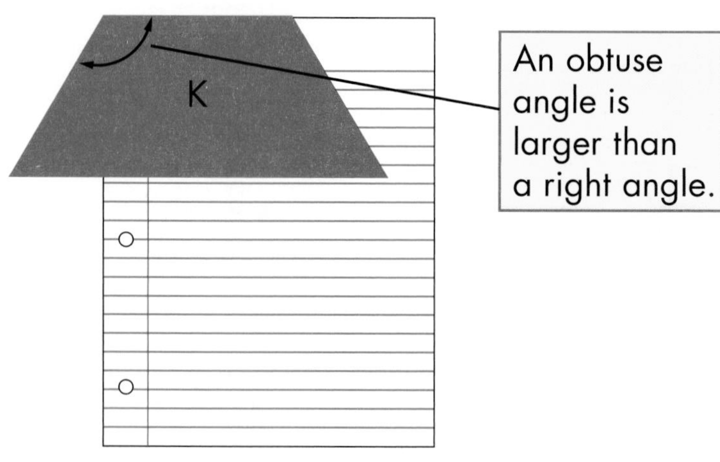
K
An obtuse angle is larger than a right angle.

Look at these figures:
Where do you see 90-degree angles?
Where do you see angles less than 90 degrees?
Where do you see angles greater than 90 degrees?

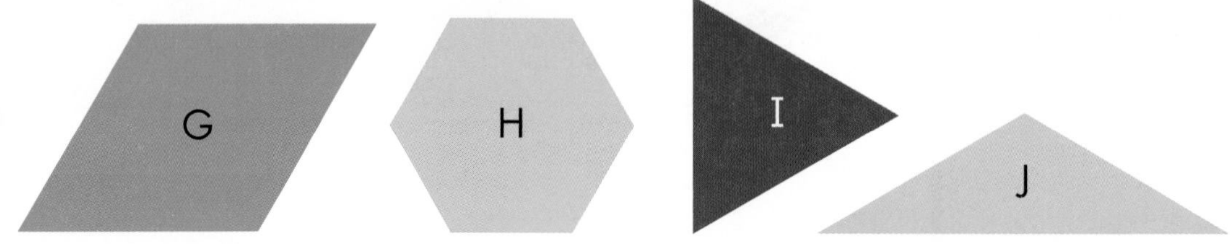
G
H
I
J

Angles (page 3 of 3)

How many degrees are in this angle?

How do you know?

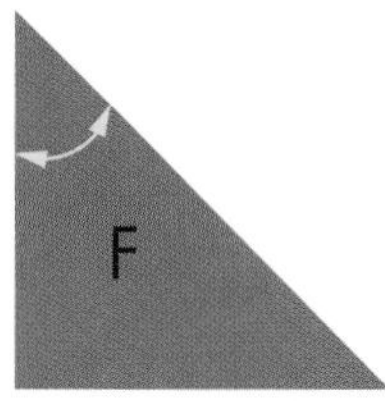

Amelia's solution

I can use two of these triangles to make a square.

$45 + 45 = 90$

These two angles together make 90°, and they are equal, so each angle measures 45°.

How many degrees are in this angle?

How do you know?

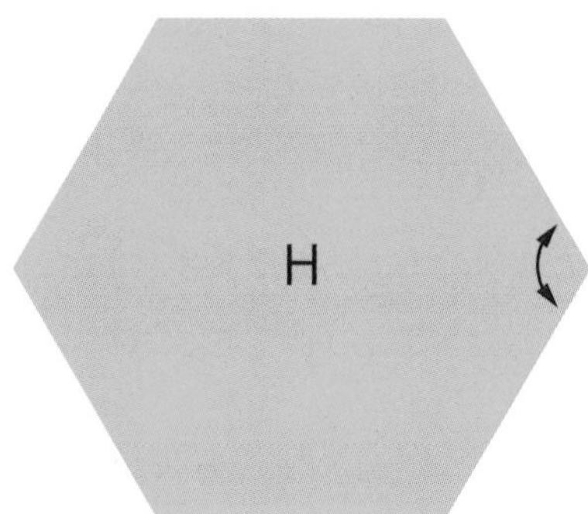

You can use the *LogoPaths* software to solve problems about angles.

Enrique's solution

When I put three of the hexagons together, three of the angles make a circle in the middle.

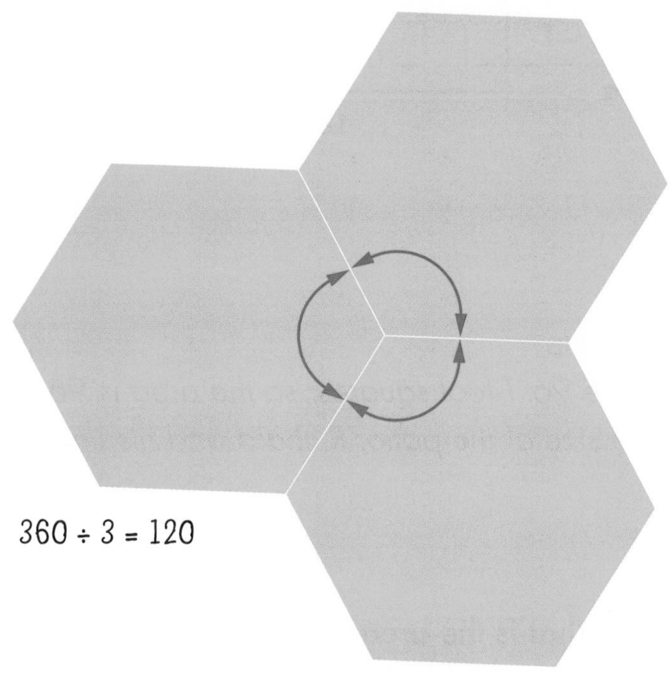

$360 \div 3 = 120$

The circle has 360°, so each angle is 120°.

How many degrees are in this angle?
How do you know?

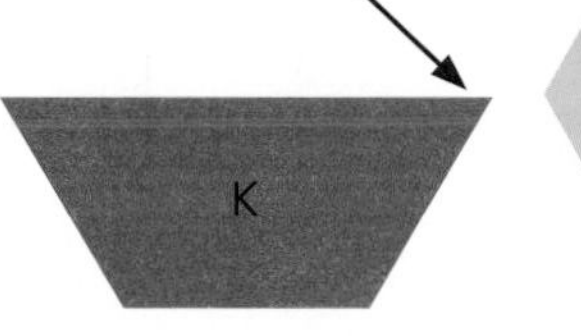

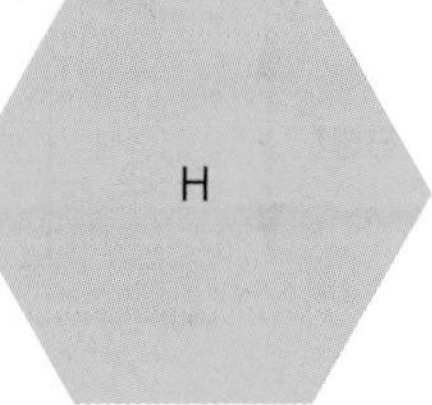

Area

Math Words
- **area**
- **square foot**

Area is the amount of surface a figure covers. Area is a measure of 2-D space.

Richard and his uncle plan to build a tiled patio. They will use square tiles, 1 foot on a side. Here is a sketch of their patio design.

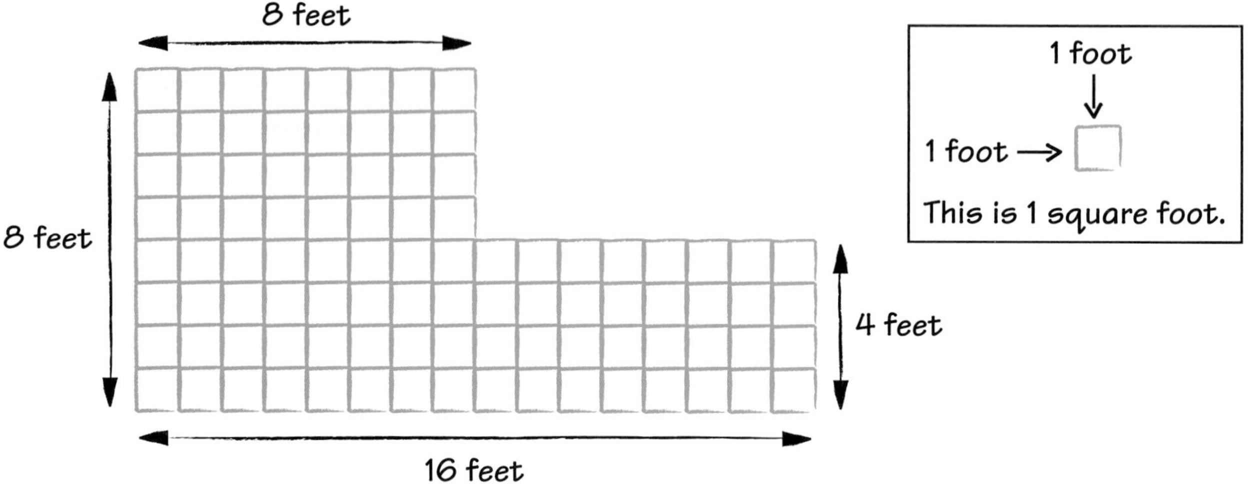

What is the area of the patio?

How many square tiles do they need?

Anna's solution

There are 96 1-foot squares, so the area is 96 square feet. That tells the size of the patio. Richard and his uncle need ***96*** *tiles.*

What is the area of this figure?

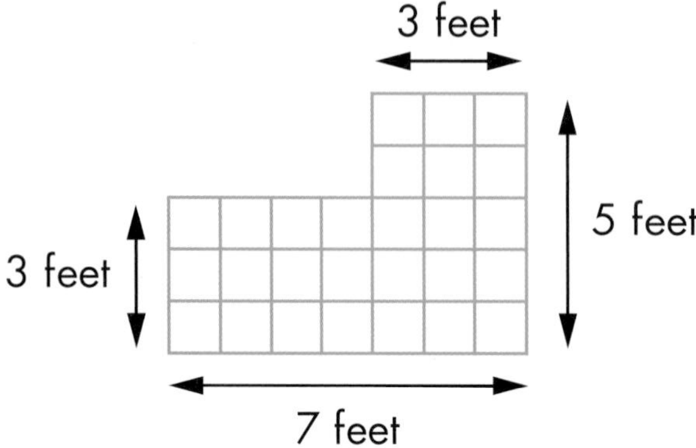

Measuring Area (page 1 of 2)

In daily life, area is often measured in square units, such as square centimeters or square feet.

Ramona built some figures on geoboards.

She counted the square units inside each figure, using squares and triangles.

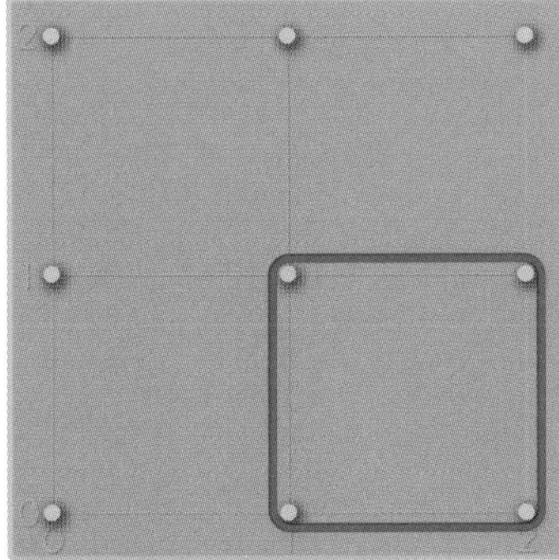

The blue square is 1 square unit.

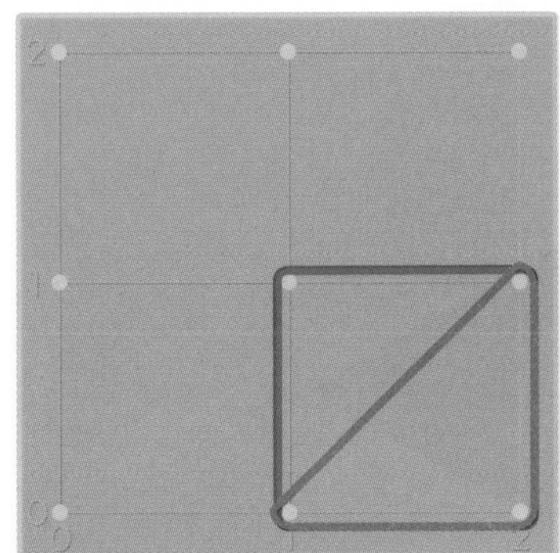

The red triangle is $\frac{1}{2}$ square unit.

1 square unit is split into 2 small triangles, so each triangle is $\frac{1}{2}$ square unit.

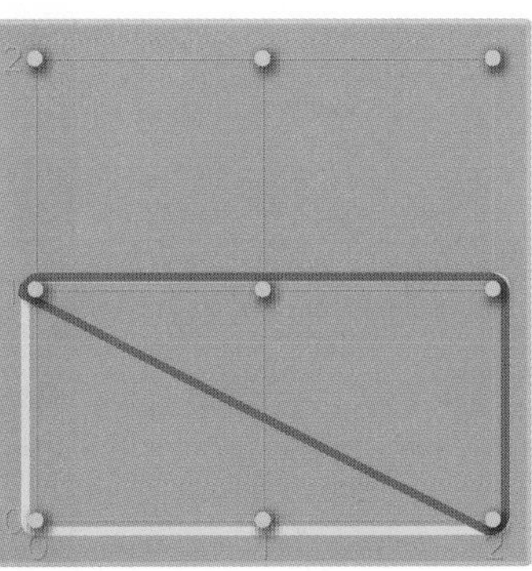

The green triangle is 1 square unit.

2 square units are split into 2 triangles, so each triangle is 1 square unit.

Ramona: *The area of all of these figures is the same. They each measure 8 square units.*

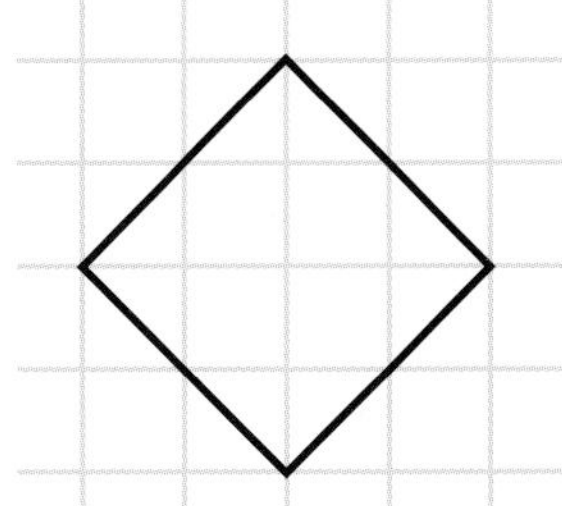

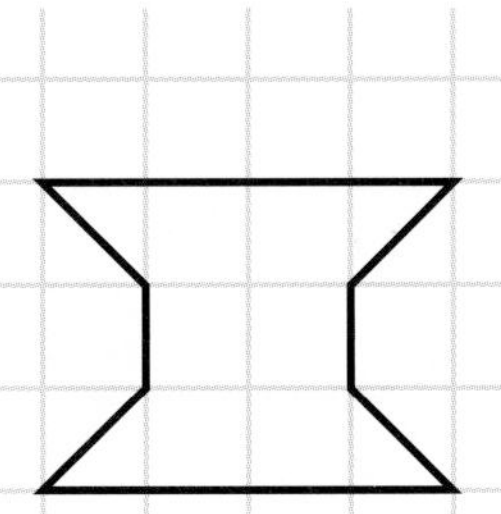

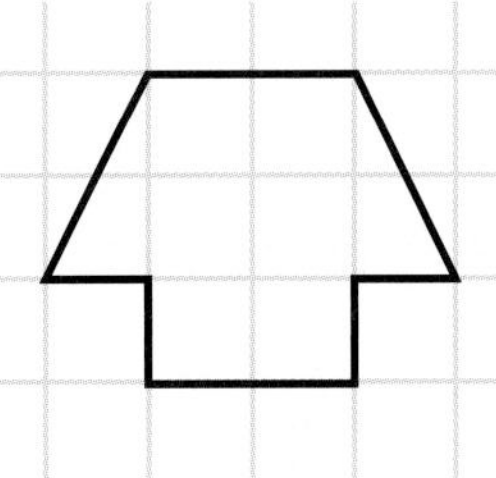

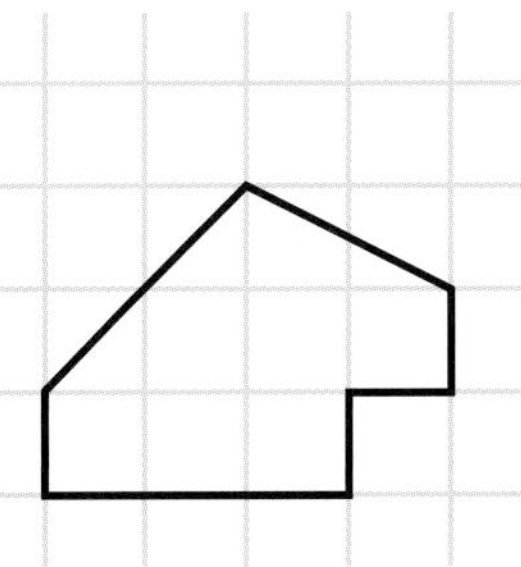

Do you agree with Ramona's statements?
Does each of these figures measure 8 square units?

Measuring Area (page 2 of 2)

While area is often measured in square units, it can also be measured with other shapes.

Anna used Power Polygons™ to build a figure.

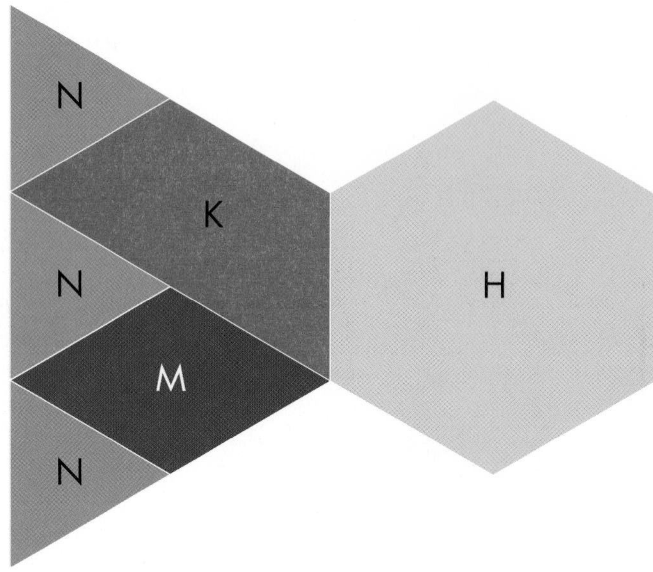

She measured the area of her figure using triangle N.

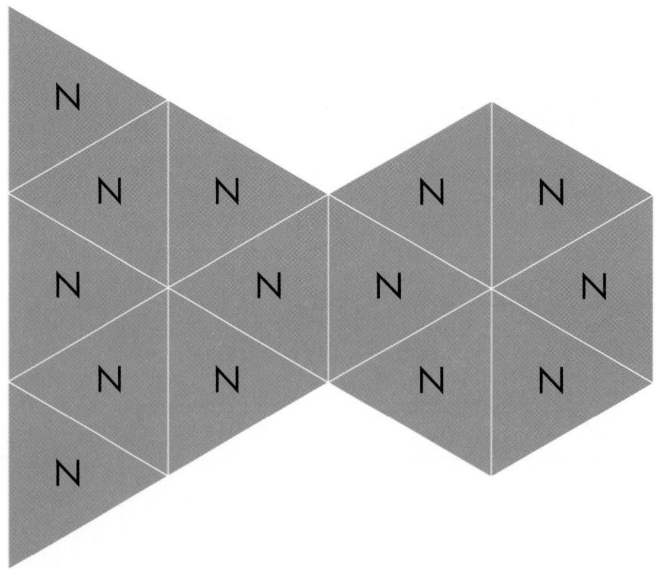

The area of my design is 14 triangle Ns.

Line Symmetry

Math Words
- **symmetry**
- **line of symmetry**

Bill and Noemi made symmetric designs using Power Polygons.

Bill: *My design has one line of symmetry. The left half of the design is the mirror image of the right half of the design.*

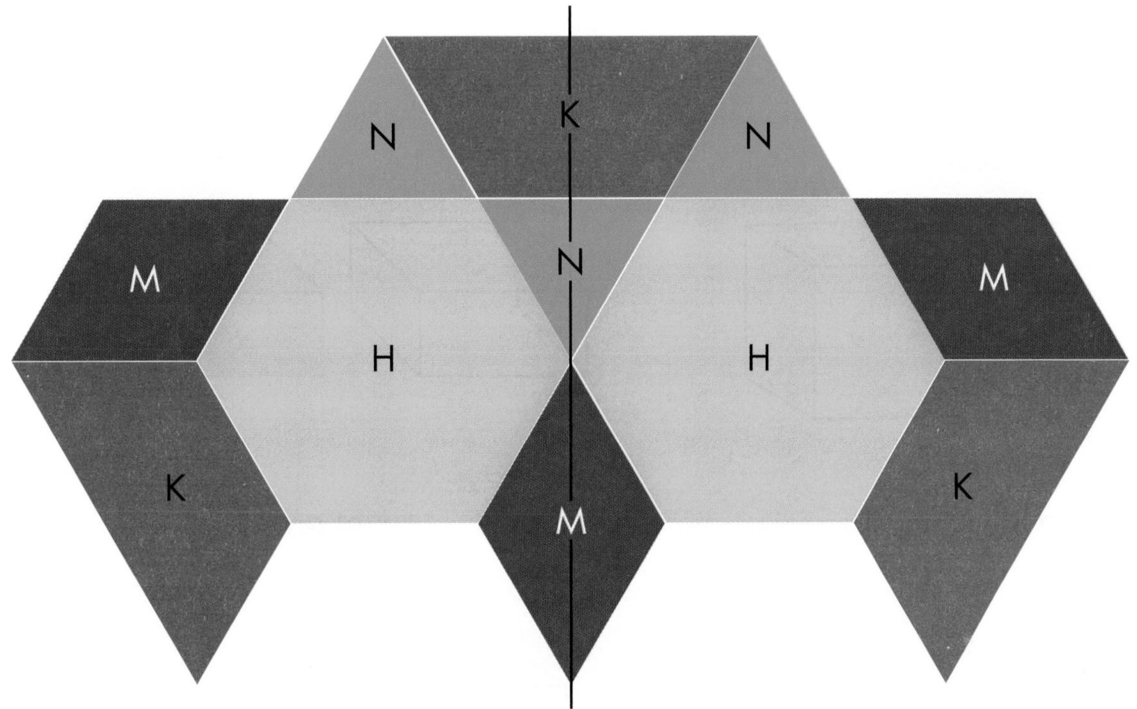

Noemi: *My design has two lines of symmetry. I can fold it up and down or side to side and the shapes will match up.*

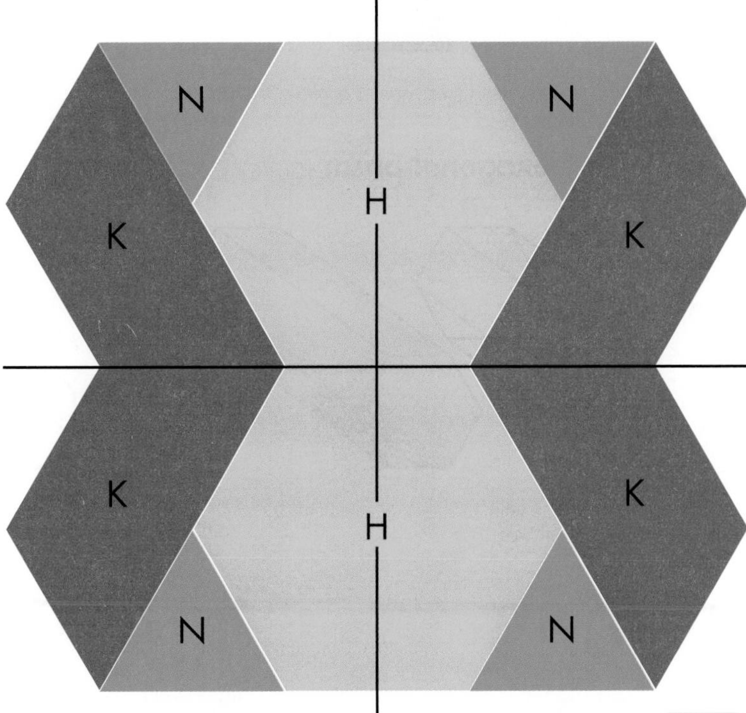

Whose design has a larger area, Bill's or Noemi's? How do you know?

Geometric Solids (page 1 of 3)

Math Words
- **geometric solid**
- **three-dimensional (3-D)**

A geometric solid is a figure that has three dimensions—length, width, and height.

Here are pictures and sketches of the set of geometric solids you are using at school.

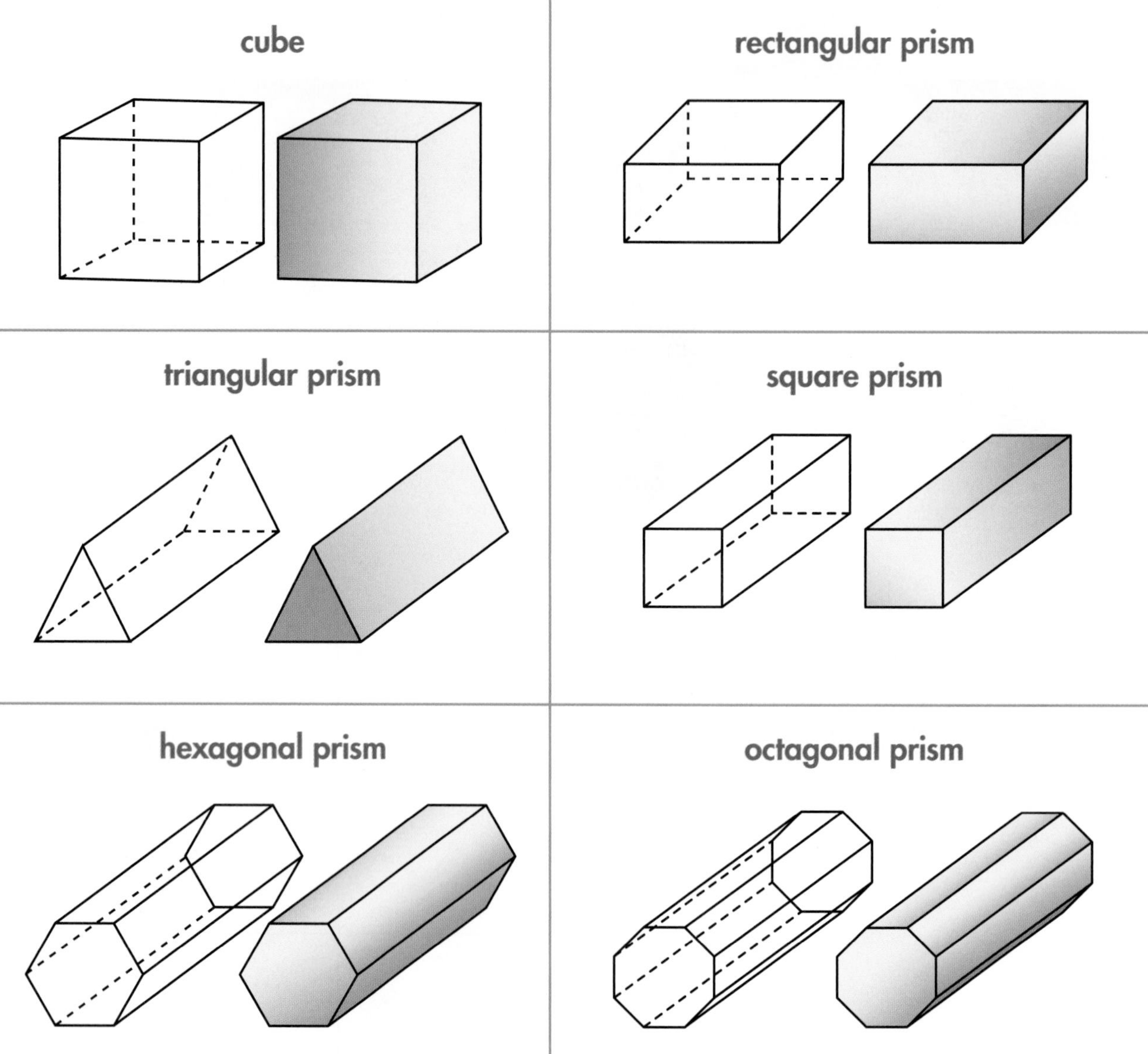

Geometric Solids (page 2 of 3)

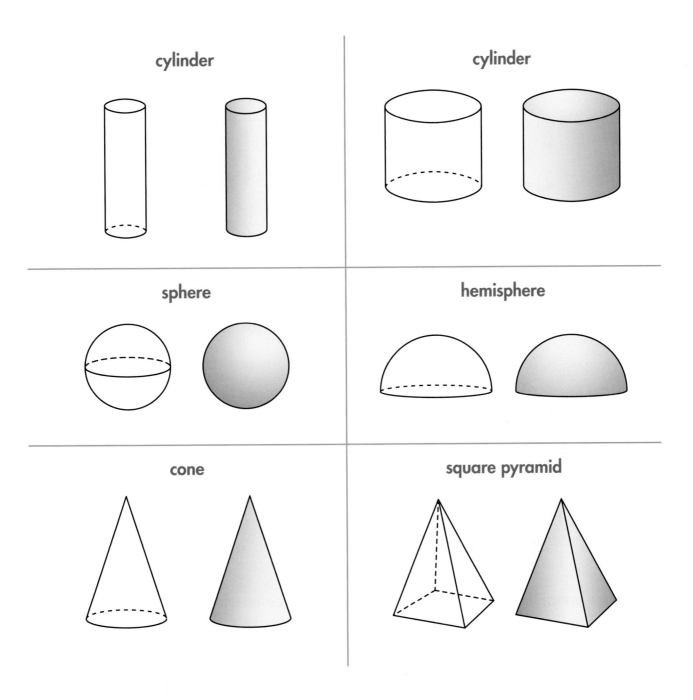

cylinder	cylinder
sphere	hemisphere
cone	square pyramid

For each geometric solid shown, describe a real-world object that has that shape.

Geometric Solids (page 3 of 3)

Lucy noticed that some objects in her kitchen looked like the solids her class had been studying in school.

Lucy: *The toaster is shaped like a rectangular prism.*

This soup can is shaped like a cylinder.

Dad's wok is shaped like a hemisphere.

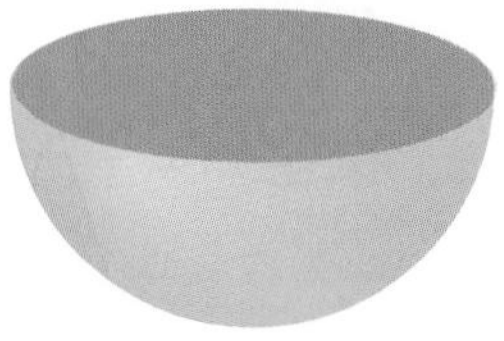

My ice cream cone is a cone and the scoop of ice cream on top looks like a sphere.

Faces, Edges, and Vertices

Math Words
- **face**
- **edge**
- **vertex (vertices)**

One way to describe a geometric solid is to identify the number of faces, edges, and vertices it has.

A face is a 2-D figure that makes up a flat surface of a 3-D solid.

An edge is the line segment where two faces meet.

A vertex is the point at the corner where edges meet.

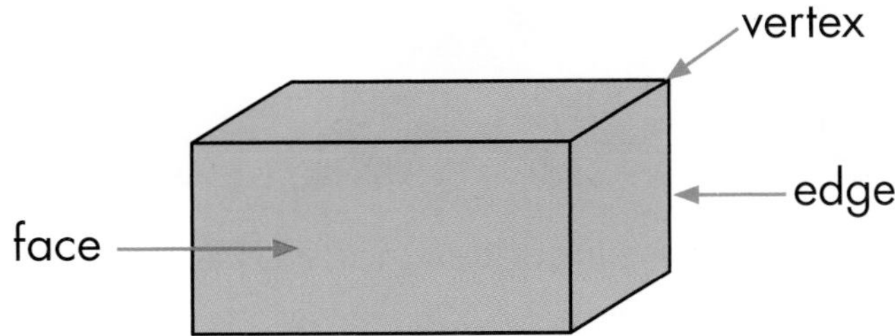

A rectangular prism has the following features:

6 faces

(You can not see all of the faces in this picture.)

12 edges

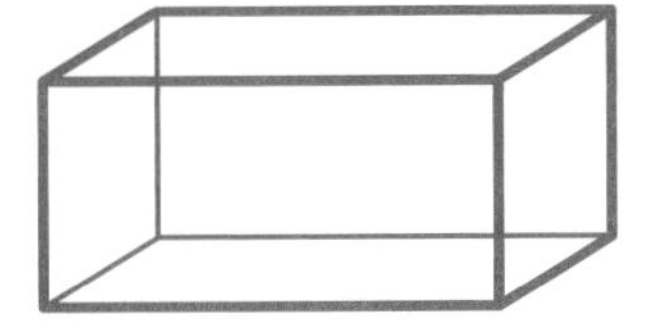

8 vertices

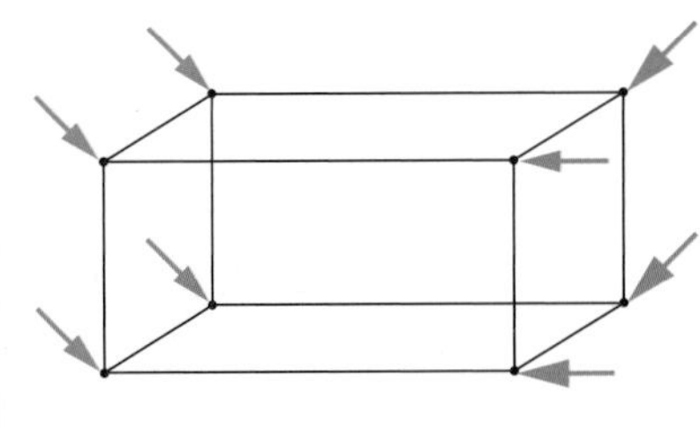

How many faces does this triangular prism have?
What do the faces look like?
How many edges does it have?
How many vertices does it have?

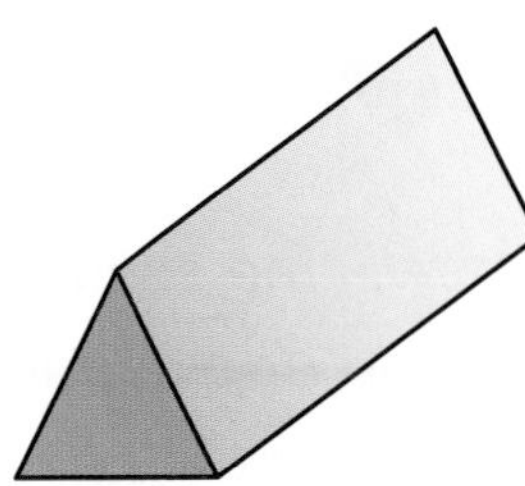

Solids and Silhouettes

(page 1 of 2)

Math Words
- **silhouette**

A silhouette is a flat, dark shape produced when an object blocks light. It is like a shadow. The light from this lamp is creating a silhouette of this girl's face. In the silhouette you can see the outline of her profile, but not the features of her face.

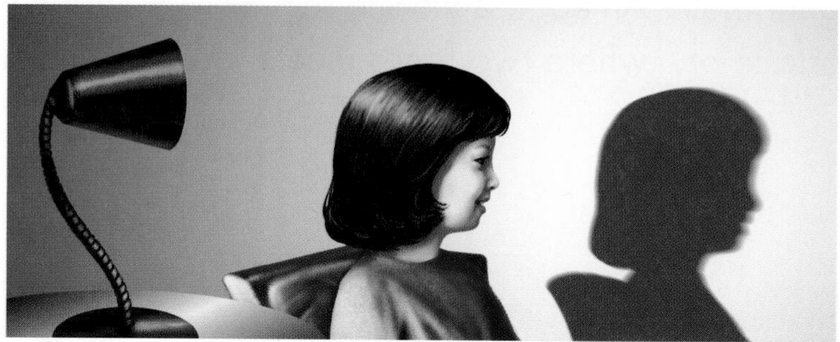

Andrew's class is examining the silhouettes made by different geometric solids.

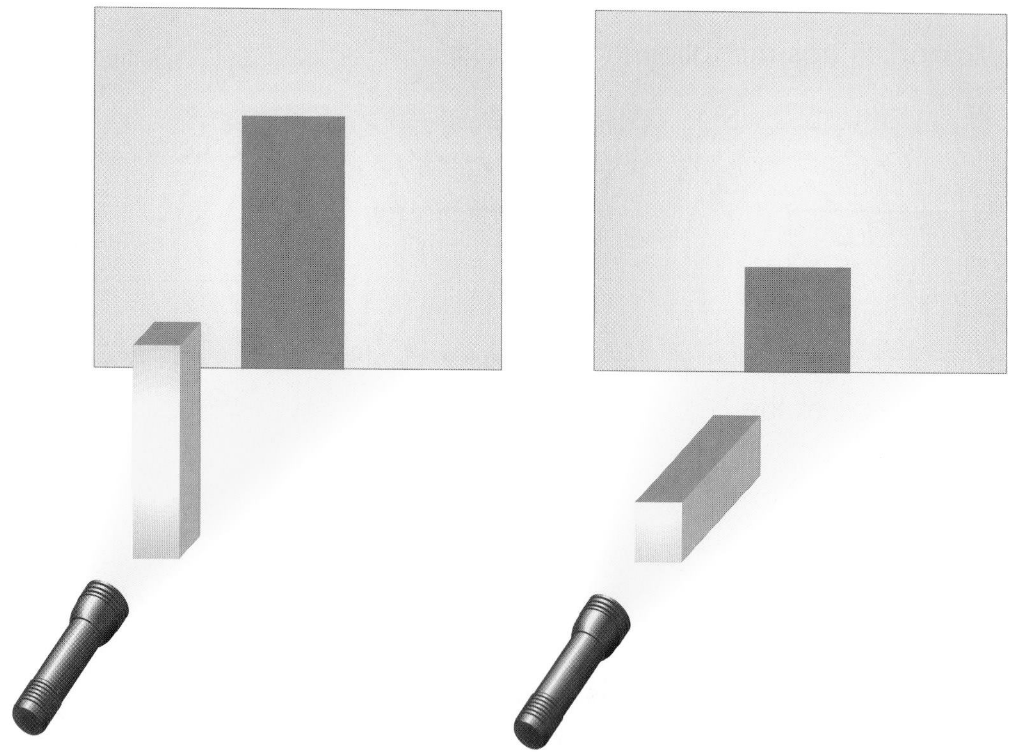

Andrew: *The square prism can make a tall, skinny rectangular silhouette or a square silhouette, depending on its position and how the light hits it.*

Solids and Silhouettes

(page 2 of 2)

Yuki: *This cylinder can make a rectangular silhouette, just as the square prism can.*

Venetta: *The surface is curved, but it makes a rectangular shadow.*

Ramona found that three different geometric solids could all make the same silhouette.

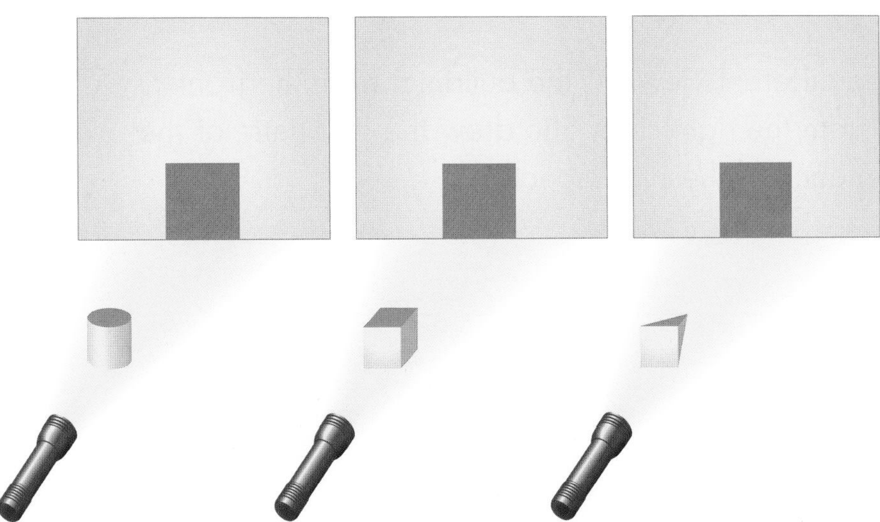

Ramona: *The cube and the square pyramid have square faces, so I expected them to have a square silhouette. The square silhouette of the wide cylinder surprised me!*

What silhouettes can this triangular prism make?

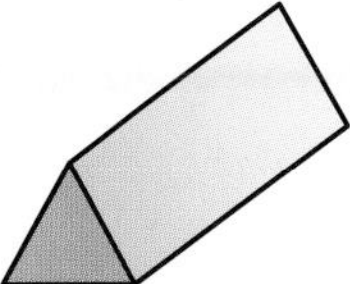

Cube Building Silhouettes

Jill used cubes to make this building.

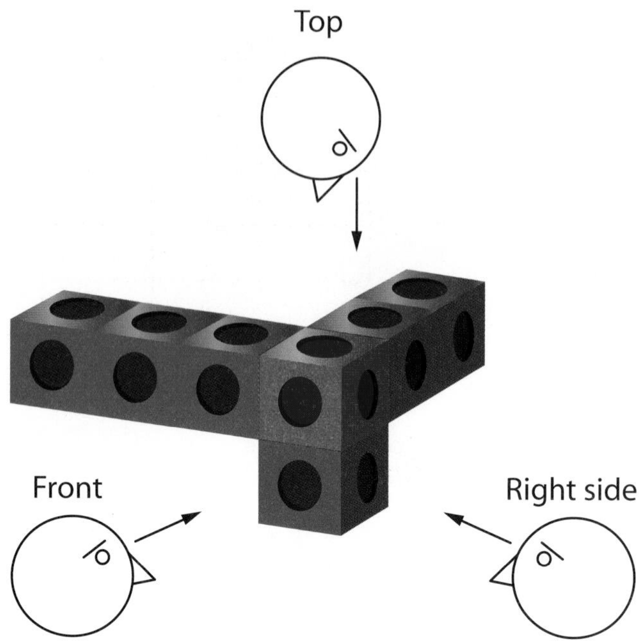

She imagined three different views of the building: from the front, from the top, and from the right side. She drew the silhouette of the cube building from each of these perspectives.

Jill's drawings

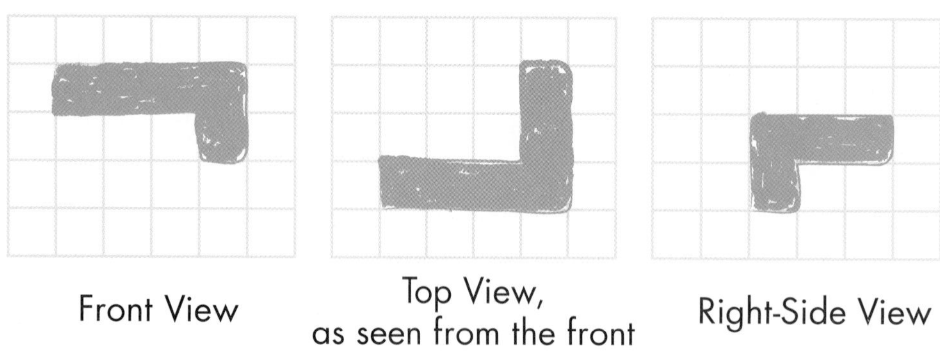

Front View | Top View, as seen from the front | Right-Side View

Where does the red cube appear in each of Jill's silhouette views?

Volume of Boxes (page 1 of 2)

Math Words
- **volume**

Volume is the amount of space a 3-D object occupies, such as the number of cubes that would completely fill a box.

Here is a pattern to make an open box.

How many cubes will fit in this box?

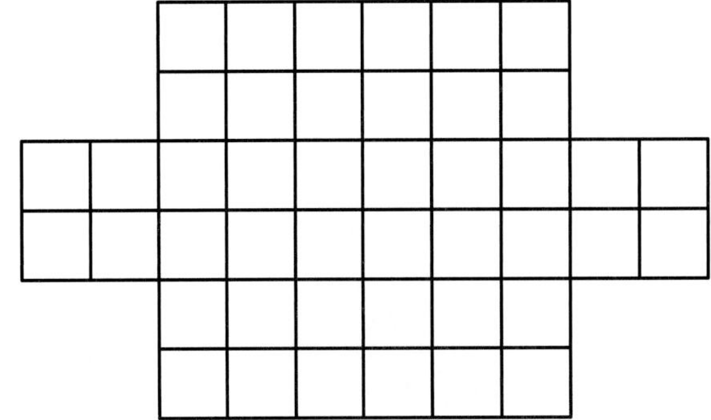

Marisol and Jake solved this problem in different ways.

Marisol: *I cut out the pattern and taped the box together. I packed the box with cubes until it was full. Then I took the cubes out and counted them.*

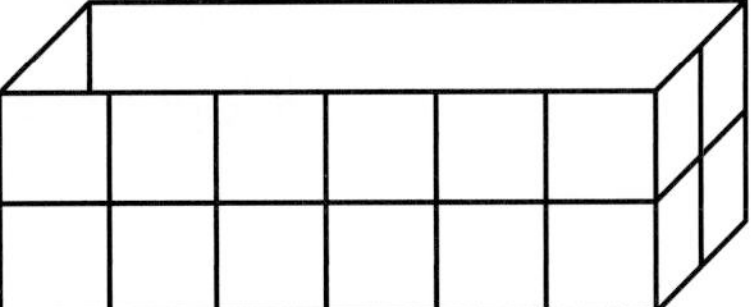

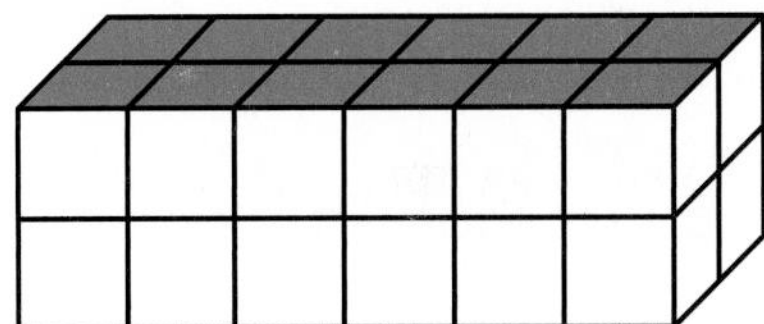

Jake: *There are 12 cubes that make the first layer of the box. When you fold up the sides of the pattern, there will be 2 layers. The box will hold 24 cubes.*

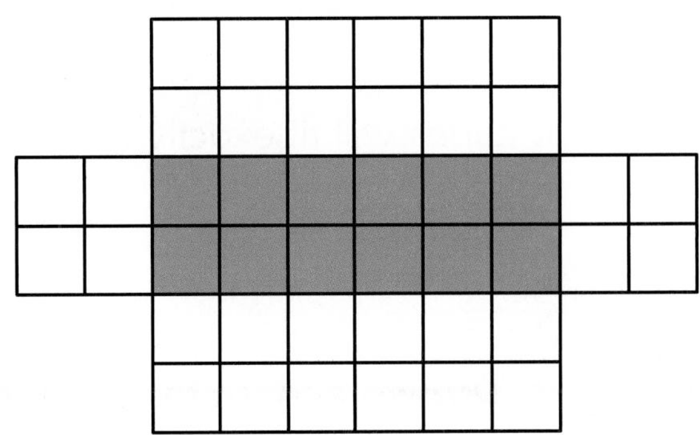

Volume of Boxes (page 2 of 2)

This is the bottom of an open box that will hold exactly 36 cubes.

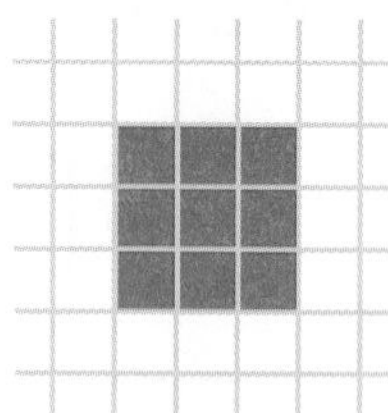

Draw the sides to complete the pattern for the box.

Andrew's solution

Nine cubes will fit on the bottom layer.
So the layers will have 9, 18, 27, 36 cubes.
That's 4 layers of 9 cubes.
I drew the sides 4 layer high.

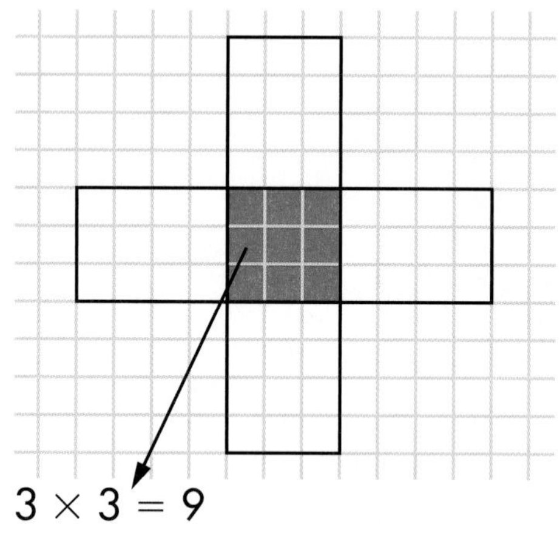

The box that Andrew designed will look like this:

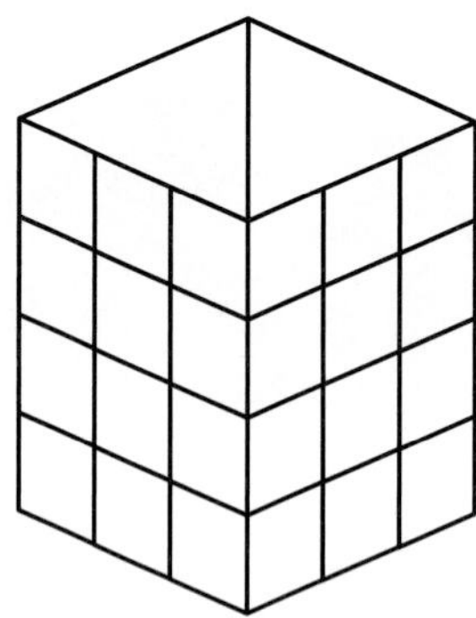

These 36 cubes will fit exactly in his box.

Draw a pattern for a different box that will also hold 36 cubes.

Games Chart

	Use in Unit	Page
Capture Fractions	6	**G1**
Changing Places	5	**G2**
Close to 1,000	5	**G3**
Decimal Compare	6	**G4**
Factor Bingo	8	**G5**
Factor Pairs	1	**G6**
Fill Two	6	**G7**
Missing Factors	3	**G8**
Multiple Turn Over	1	**G9**
Small Array/Big Array	3	**G10**

Capture Fractions

You need

- deck of Fraction Cards

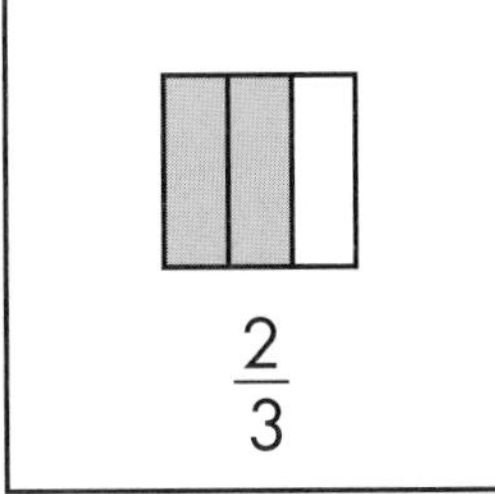

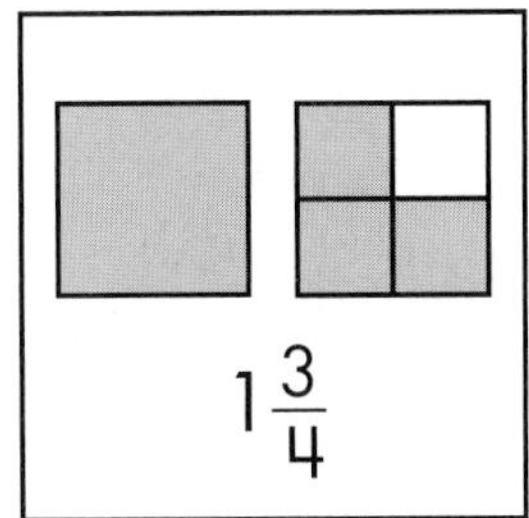

Play with a partner or a small group.

1. Divide the deck into equal-sized piles, one for each player. Players place their cards facedown.
2. In each round, each player turns over the top card in his or her pile. The player with the largest fraction wins, takes the other players' cards, and puts them on the bottom of his or her own pile.
3. If two of the cards show equivalent fractions, those two players turn over another card. Whoever has the larger fraction wins all the other players' cards.
4. The person with the most cards wins. The game can be stopped at any time.

Changing Places

You need

- 1,000 book
- Change Cards
- *Changing Places* Recording Sheet

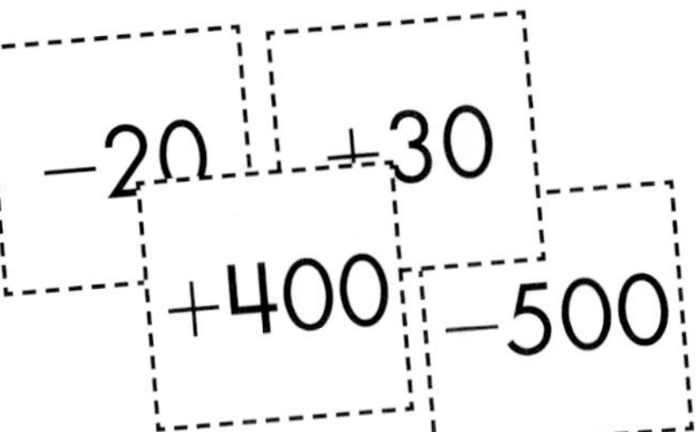

Name Date

Landmarks and Large Numbers

Changing Places Recording Sheet

Record your starting number, the Change Cards you used, and an equation that shows the new number you made.

Remember that your new number is always your next starting number!

Starting Number	Change Cards	Equation
Example: 243	+10, −20, +100	243 + 10 − 20 + 100 = 333
1.		
2.		
3.		
4.		
5.		
6.		
7.		
8.		
9.		
10.		

Session 1.3 Unit 5 5

Play with a partner.

1. Choose a page from your 1,000 book and write a new number of your choice on that page. This will be your starting number.
2. Draw five Change Cards from the set and spread them faceup so that you and your partner can see them. You will both use the same set of cards for each round.
3. Use any or all of the Change Cards to make a new number to write in your 1,000 book. If the number you make is already written in, find a different way to use the Change Cards.
4. If for some reason you cannot use the Change Cards that have been drawn to write a new number on the page you have chosen, you may replace them with new cards.
5. On your next round, draw five new Change Cards. For your starting number, use the number you just wrote in your book.
6. For each round, check to make sure that your set of changes works. Record the equation that shows your starting number, the Change Cards you used, and your new number on the *Changing Places* Recording Sheet.

Variation

Use the 10,000 chart your class made and the Changing Places on the 10,000 Chart sheet. (Your teacher will provide extra copies as needed.) Follow the directions on the sheet to find new numbers. Write the new numbers on the 10,000 chart.

Close to 1,000

You need

- Digit Cards (1 deck per pair)
- *Close to 1,000* Recording Sheet

Name Date
Landmarks and Large Numbers

Close to 1,000 Recording Sheet

Game 1		Score
Round 1:	___ + ___ =	___
Round 2:	___ + ___ =	___
Round 3:	___ + ___ =	___
Round 4:	___ + ___ =	___
Round 5:	___ + ___ =	___
	Final Score	___

Game 2		Score
Round 1:	___ + ___ =	___
Round 2:	___ + ___ =	___
Round 3:	___ + ___ =	___
Round 4:	___ + ___ =	___
Round 5:	___ + ___ =	___
	Final Score	___

M22 Unit 5 Sessions 2.5, 2.6, 3.4, 3.5, 4.2, 4.3, 4.5, 4.6

Play with a partner.

1. Deal out eight Digit Cards to each player.
2. Use any six cards to make two numbers. For example, a 6, a 5, and a 2 could make 652, 625, 526, 562, 256, or 265. Wild cards can be used as any digit. Try to make two numbers that, when added together, give you a total that is close to 1,000.
3. Write these numbers and their total on the *Close to 1,000* Recording Sheet. For example, 652 + 347 = 999.
4. Find your score. Your score is the difference between your total and 1,000.
5. Put the cards you used in a discard pile. Keep the two cards you did not use for the next round.
6. For the next round, deal six cards to each player. Make more numbers that have a sum close to 1,000.
7. When you run out of cards, mix up the discard pile and use them again.
8. After five rounds, add your scores to find your final score. The player with the lower final score wins.

Variation

Write the score with plus and minus signs to show whether your total is less than or greater than 1,000. For example, if your total is 999, your score is −1. If your total is 1,005, your score is +5. The total of these two scores is +4. Your goal is to get a final score for five rounds that is as close to 0 as possible.

Decimal Compare

You need

- deck of Decimal Cards (2 decks can be combined if 3–4 people play.)

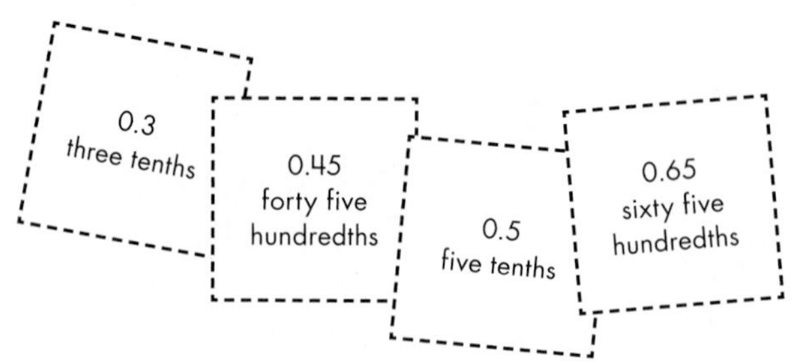

Play with 2 or more players.

1. Divide the deck into equal piles, one for each player. Players place their cards facedown.

2. In each round, each player turns over the top card in his or her pile. The player with the largest number wins, takes the other players' cards, and puts them on the bottom of his or her own pile.

3. If two of the cards show the same number (when 2 decks are combined), those two players turn over another card. Whoever has the larger number wins all the other players' cards.

4. The person with the most cards wins. The game can be stopped at any time.

Factor Bingo

630

180

You need

- Number Cards for *Factor Bingo* (1 deck per pair)
- *Factor Bingo* Gameboards (1 per player)
- counters or pennies to cover the numbers

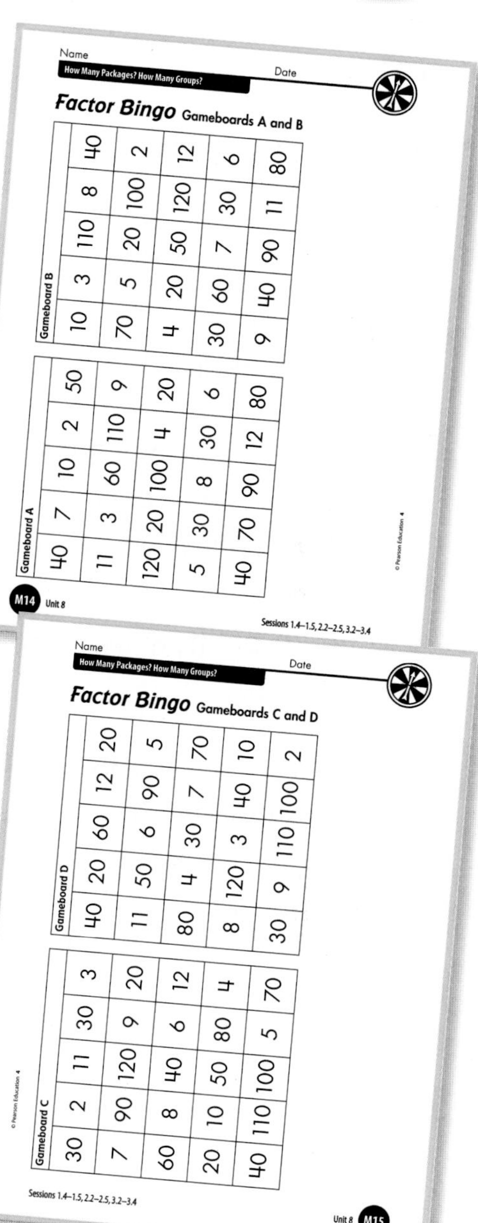

Name Date

How Many Packages? How Many Groups?

Factor Bingo Gameboards A and B

Gameboard B

10	3	110	8	40
70	5	20	100	2
4	20	50	120	12
30	60	7	30	6
9	40	90	11	80

Gameboard A

40	7	10	2	50
11	3	60	110	9
120	20	100	4	20
5	30	8	30	6
40	70	90	12	80

M14 Unit 8 Sessions 1.4–1.5, 2.2–2.5, 3.2–3.4

© Pearson Education 4

Name Date

How Many Packages? How Many Groups?

Factor Bingo Gameboards C and D

Gameboard D

40	20	60	12	20
11	50	6	90	5
80	4	30	7	70
8	120	3	40	10
30	9	110	100	2

Gameboard C

30	2	11	30	3
7	90	120	9	20
60	8	40	6	12
20	10	50	80	4
40	110	100	5	70

© Pearson Education 4

Sessions 1.4–1.5, 2.2–2.5, 3.2–3.4 Unit 8 M15

Play with a partner.

1. Each player chooses one of the four *Factor Bingo* gameboards. Players play on different gameboards. For example, one player chooses Gameboard A and the other player chooses Gameboard B for the first game.
2. The first player draws a card from the deck of Number Cards for *Factor Bingo.* Each player looks at his or her gameboard and chooses one number that is a factor of the number on the card. Players cover that factor with a counter. Players can choose different factors.
3. The second player draws a card, and again players choose a factor of that number on their own gameboards and cover the factor with a counter.
4. If a player draws a Wild Card, the player says any number that is a multiple of 10, and all players must then find a factor of that number on their gameboards.
5. The game is over when one player has covered five numbers in a row, either vertically, horizontally, or diagonally.

Factor Pairs

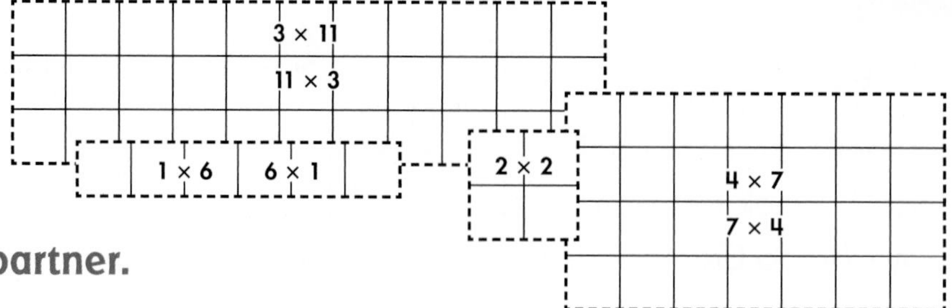

You need

- set of Array Cards

Play alone or with a partner.

1. Spread out all of the Array Cards in front of you. All cards should have the dimensions side faceup.

2. Choose an Array Card and put your finger on it. Say the number of squares in the array if you know it. (Don't pick up the card until you say the answer.) If you don't know the number of squares, use a strategy to figure it out. Find a way to figure out how many squares there are without counting every one.

3. Turn the card over to check your answer. If your answer is correct, then you get to keep the card.

4. If you are playing with a partner, take turns choosing cards and finding the number of squares in each array.

5. The game is over when you have picked up all the cards.

6. While you are playing, make lists for yourself of "Combinations I Know" and "Combinations I'm Working On." You'll be using these lists to help you learn your multiplication combinations.

Fill Two

0.75 seventy five hundredths

0.1 one tenth

0.9 nine tenths

You need

- deck of Decimal Cards
- 10 × 10 squares, 1 sheet per player
- Crayons or markers (two or more colors) for each player

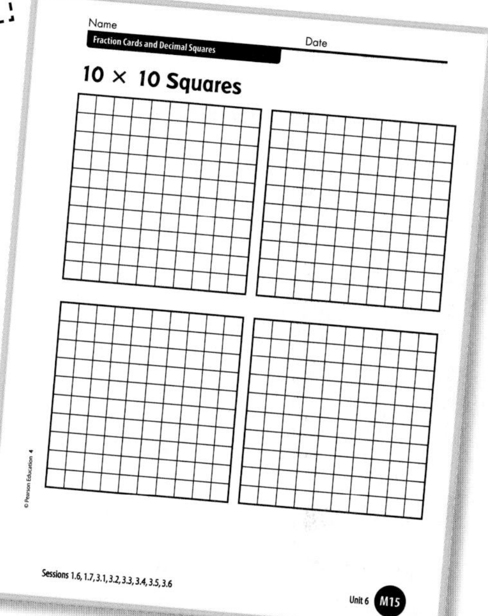

Play with a partner.

1. Mix the cards and place the deck facedown. Turn over the top four cards and place them faceup in a row.
2. Player 1 chooses one of the faceup cards, colors in that amount on one of the squares on the 10 × 10 squares sheet, and writes the decimal number below the square. The goal is to shade in two of the squares as completely as possible. A player may never color in an amount that would more than fill a square, and may not split an amount to color in parts of two squares.
3. After one of the four cards has been picked, replace it with the top card from the deck. Player 2 then chooses one of the faceup cards and goes through the same steps.
4. Change colors for each turn so that players can see the different decimal numbers. As the players write the numbers below each square, they use plus (+) signs between the decimals, making an equation that will show the total colored in on each square.
5. If all cards showing are greater than the spaces left on a player's square, the player loses his or her turn until a card that he or she can use is turned up.
6. The game is over when neither player can play a card. Players add all of the numbers they have colored in on each square, and combine those sums to get a final total for both squares. The winner is the player whose final sum is closest to 2.

Missing Factors

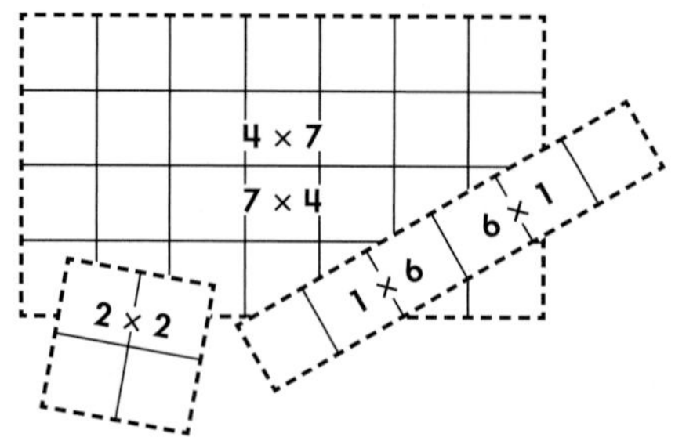

You need

- set of Array Cards
- *Missing Factors* Recording Sheet

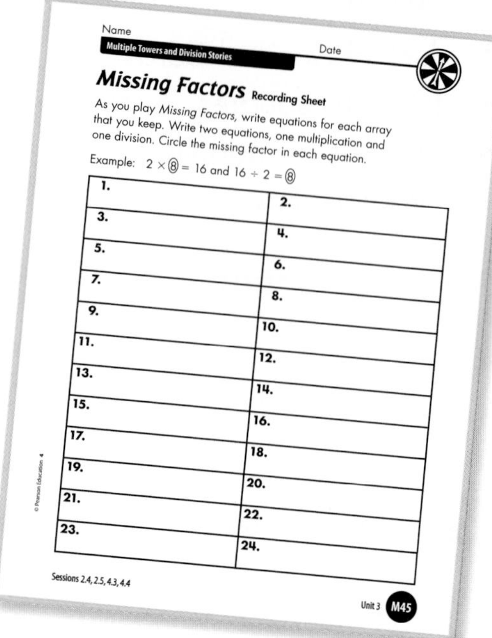

Name Date

Multiple Towers and Division Stories

Missing Factors Recording Sheet

As you play *Missing Factors*, write equations for each array that you keep. Write two equations, one multiplication and one division. Circle the missing factor in each equation.

Example: $2 \times (8) = 16$ and $16 \div 2 = (8)$

1.	2.
3.	4.
5.	6.
7.	8.
9.	10.
11.	12.
13.	14.
15.	16.
17.	18.
19.	20.
21.	22.
23.	24.

Sessions 2.4, 2.5, 4.3, 4.4

Unit 3 M45

Play alone or with a partner.

1. Spread out all the Array Cards in front of you, with the product side showing.
2. Choose an Array Card. One dimension is given. Your job is to say what the other dimension is. This is the missing factor. For example, if you choose an Array Card that has a total of 16, and one dimension is 2, the missing factor is 8.
3. Turn the card over to check your answer. If your answer is correct, keep the card. If your answer is not correct, return the card to the set of Array Cards, factor side up.
4. On the *Missing Factors* Recording Sheet, write two equations, one multiplication equation and one division equation, to go with each array you keep. Circle the missing factor. For example:

   $2 \times (8) = 16$ and $16 \div 2 = (8)$
5. If you are playing with a partner, take turns choosing cards until all of the cards with products still showing have been picked up.
6. When there are cards with only factors sides showing, take turns pointing to a card and saying what is on the other side (the total number of squares), keeping the cards when your answers are correct. The player with the most cards wins.

Multiple Turn Over

You need

- deck of Multiple Cards
- calculators (optional)
- *Multiple Turn Over* Recording Sheet

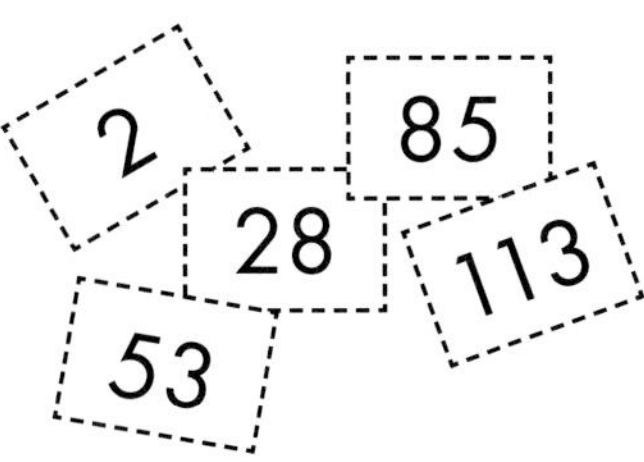

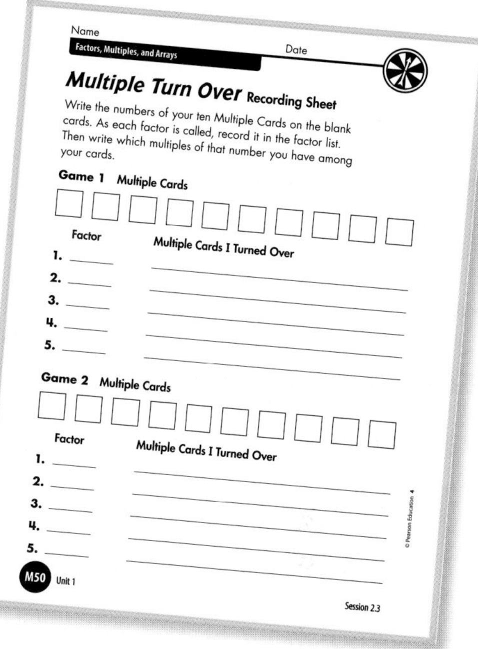

Name Date

Factors, Multiples, and Arrays

Multiple Turn Over Recording Sheet

Write the numbers of your ten Multiple Cards on the blank cards. As each factor is called, record it in the factor list. Then write which multiples of that number you have among your cards.

Game 1 Multiple Cards

Factor Multiple Cards I Turned Over

1. ____
2. ____
3. ____
4. ____
5. ____

Game 2 Multiple Cards

Factor Multiple Cards I Turned Over

1. ____
2. ____
3. ____
4. ____
5. ____

M50 Unit 1 Session 2.3

Basic Game: Numbers 2–50
Intermediate Game: Numbers 2–80
Advanced Game: Numbers 2–113

Play with a partner or in a small group.

1. Deal out ten Multiple Cards to each player.
2. Players arrange their Multiple Cards faceup in front of them. Each player should be able to see everyone's Multiple Cards.
3. The player with the smallest multiple begins. This player calls out any whole number (except 1). Each player records that factor on his or her *Multiple Turn Over* Recording Sheet.
4. All the players (including the player who called out the number) search for cards in their set that are multiples of that number. They write those multiples on their recording sheet and turn those cards facedown. If a player has no multiples of a number called, that player writes "none" under "Multiple Cards I Turned Over."
5. Players take turns calling out numbers. The game is over when one player turns over all ten Multiple Cards.

Small Array/Big Array

(page 1 of 2)

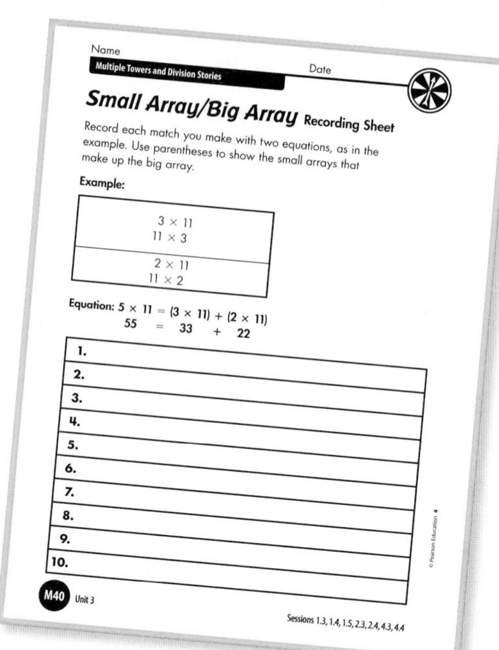

Name Date

Multiple Towers and Division Stories

Small Array/Big Array Recording Sheet

Record each match you make with two equations, as in the example. Use parentheses to show the small arrays that make up the big array.

Example:

3×11 11×3
2×11 11×2

Equation: $5 \times 11 = (3 \times 11) + (2 \times 11)$
$55 = 33 + 22$

1.
2.
3.
4.
5.
6.
7.
8.
9.
10.

© Pearson Education 4

M40 Unit 3

Sessions 1.3, 1.4, 1.5, 2.3, 2.4, 4.3, 4.4

You need

- set of Array Cards
- *Small Array/Big Array* Recording Sheet
- construction paper

Play with a partner, or form 2-player teams and play each other.

1. Deal out 10 Array Cards to each player (or team) and spread them out, factor side up.
2. On a sheet of construction paper, spread out 6 more Array Cards, factor side up. These are the center cards. Place the remaining cards in a pile to one side.
3. Players take turns matching small arrays to big arrays. "Matching" means that both arrays have one dimension, or one whole side, that is the same. For example, 3×11 and 5×11 are a match.
4. On your turn, try to match one of your Array Cards to a center card. Place your card on top of the center card so that it covers part of the array. You may play only one array on a turn.

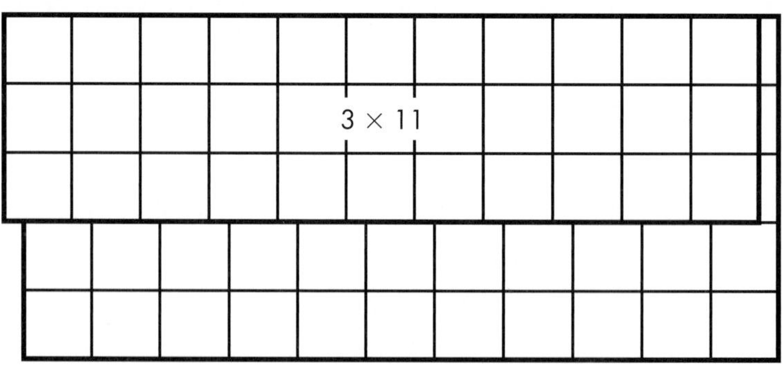

Small Array/Big Array

(page 2 of 2)

5. If none of your Array Cards matches a center card, you may do one of these two things:

   (a) Draw a card from the pile. Play it if you can, or add it to your Array Cards if you cannot.

   (b) Choose one center array that matches another center array, and play that card. This is particularly useful when there are small arrays in the center.

6. If you use a center array to cover another center array, you must either

   (a) replace it with a card from the pile; or

   (b) put one of your own Array Cards in the center. There must always be 6 cards in the center.

7. The goal is to make a complete match by covering a big array with a combination of 2 or 3 smaller arrays. When you play a card that makes a complete match, you collect both the big array and the smaller arrays covering it. Then you replace the center card with one from the pile. On the *Small Array/Big Array* Recording Sheet, use equations to record the complete match, using parentheses to show the smaller arrays. For example:

   $5 \times 11 = (3 \times 11) + (2 \times 11)$

   $55 = 33 + 22$

8. Keep in mind that there is only one card for each array. Sometimes, to complete a match, you need an array that has already been used. When this happens, you may use your turn to say what the needed card is and complete the match.

9. The game is over when there are no more cards or no more matches can be made.

Illustrations

16–18, 44–46, 49–64, 102–111, 122–123 Jonathan Massie
36, 98, 123 Thomas Gagliano
48, 101, 122 Jared Osterhold
71–86, 99, 102 Jeff Grunewald

Photographs

Every effort has been made to secure permission and provide appropriate credit for photographic material. The publisher deeply regrets any omission and pledges to correct errors called to its attention in subsequent editions.

Unless otherwise acknowledged, all photographs are the property of Scott Foresman, a division of Pearson Education.

Photo locators denoted as follows: Top (T), Center (C), Bottom (B), Left (L), Right (R), Background (Bkgd)

Cover Karin Kuhlmann/©Artists Rights Society (ARS); **7** ©Hot Ideas/Index Open; **11** (B) Dirk Anschutz/Getty Images, (T) Getty Images; **53** Jupiter Images; **54** SuperStock; **76** Tim de Waele/Corbis; **101** (CL) Getty Images, (BR) Michael Waine/Corbis, (C) Peter Gardner/©DK Images, (BL) Jupiter Images; **109** ©Royalty-Free/Corbis; **111** Jupiter Images; **120** (BL) Oliver Eltinger/Corbis, (CL) Dave King/©DK Images, (TL) Jupiter Images